THE NEW ILLUSTRATED GUIDE TO
MODERN
RIFLES
& SUB-MACHINE GUNS

MAJOR FREDERICK MYATT M.C.
& GERARD RIDEFORT

THE NEW ILLUSTRATED GUIDE TO
MODERN
RIFLES
& SUB-MACHINE GUNS

SMITHMARK

A Salamander Book

©Salamander Books Ltd 1992., 129-137 York Way, London N7 9LG, U.K.

ISBN 0-8317-5055-3

This edition published in 1992 by SMITHMARK Publishers Inc., 112 Madison Avenue, New York, NY 10016.

SMITHMARK books are available for bulk purchase for sales promotion and premium use. For details write or telephone the Manager of Special Sales, SMITHMARK Publishers Inc., 112 Madison Avenue, New York, NY 10016. (212) 532-6600.

Contents

Credits

Authors: Major Frederick Myatt, M.C., is a former curator of the Weapons Museum, School of Infantry, Warminster.

Gerard Ridefort has spent all his adult life in military service; a career which has included the commanding of special forces units.

Original Consultant: Colonel John Weeks, internationally recognised expert on weaponry and author of several military firearms' books.

Editors: Chris Westhorp and Richard O'Neill.
Designers: Tim Scott and Barry Savage.
Weapons photography: Barry Scott ©Salamander Books Ltd.
Photographs: Full credits on page 158.
Filmset: The Old Mill, England and Modern Text Ltd, England.
Color reproduction: Scantrans PTE, Singapore.
Printed in Hong Kong.

The Rifle and Carbine

A body of Swiss conscripts armed with 7.5mm Sturmgewehr 57 rifles which they keep at home. More recent recruits have been equipped with the 5.6mm Sturmgewehr 90.

Rifled firearms, in which slow, spiral, parallel grooves cut into the bore impart spin to the projectile and give it a considerable degree of stability in flight, existed as early as the 16th century. They were, however, both expensive to make and very slow to load, since a tight-fitting lead sphere had to be forced down the full length of the barrel from the muzzle end. Thus, the rifle remained for many years a weapon mainly for wealthy sportsmen and game shooters.

It is thought that a few rifles, then called "screwed guns", were used as sniper-type arms during the English Civil Wars (1642-51), but probably the first to make wide use of rifled arms were the frontiersmen of North America, who relied on game-shooting for food and other necessities. There evolved a characteristic "long

Above: *A firing line of British Army Gurkhas in 1885 gives an impression of the firepower obtained from massed ranks. Their Enfield rifles are fitted with the Snider hinged-block breech.*

Below: *British infantrymen dismount from their Warrior fighting vehicles armed with the shorter L85A1 which is better suited than the L1A1 to the confined spaces offered by battlefield transportation.*

rifle'', with a barrel length of up to 4ft (1299mm) and a calibre of around 0.5in (12mm). Reloading was speeded up by wrapping the ball in a circular patch of oiled leather or linen.

During the 18th century, the American colonists' rifles proved their worth against the Indians; against the French in the Seven Years' War (1756-63); and against British regulars during the American Revolution of 1775-83 — when the British also made effective use of the Ferguson breechloading rifle.

Rifles in 19th Century Warfare

The rifle's value as a specialist arm was apparent to many British officers who had served in America — and the French use of skirmishers to precede their attacking columns during the Revolutionary Wars necessitated the use of similar troops in opposition. In 1800, therefore, the British Army raised a Rifle Regiment armed with the Baker flintlock, which shot fairly well to 300yds (274m). In the 1850s, reloading speed was much improved by the adoption, first, of the French-developed Minié rifle — taking an elongated projectile with a hollow base, which expanded the lead bullet into the rifling *after* it had been rammed down — and then of the Enfield rifle.

The Enfield, although still loading at only about two rounds per minute, shot well to c880yds (805m) in expert hands, dramatically increasing the effective fire zone of infantry in defence. Most of the world's modern armies were soon equipped with similar weapons. Their effect on tactics, evident in the American Civil War (1861-65), was profound: battles became more open and started at greater ranges; frontal attacks became suicidal; defensive works, ie, trenches, were essential; and the roles of cavalry and horse artillery were radically changed and limited.

But most European powers clung to their percussion muzzle-loaders in spite of the obvious need for effective breechloaders. Although Prussia developed the ''needle-gun'' — a single shot, bolt-action rifle firing a non-metallic consumable cartridge — in the 1840s, the arm was not widely taken up. Nevertheless, Prussian victories over the Danes (1864), the Austrians (1866) and the French (in 1870; when the French Army had a superior needle-gun type, the Chassepot, but failed to derive a tactical advantage), led to general acceptance of the single-shot, bolt-action rifle firing self-contained cartridges. Rate of fire was increased by such devices as the Snider hinged-block breech — the Martini-Henry falling-block breech rifle was in general British issue by c1874 — but these were soon superseded by rifles with tubular or box magazines, using smokeless powder.

The Development of Automatic Weapons

Modern soldiers are equipped with rifles very distinct from those used before. The infantrymen of today's major armies fight from armoured vehicles, dismounting to attack the enemy under cover of machine-gun and cannon fire from their own combat vehicles. The infantryman's rifle must be short and handy enough for him to leap from a vehicle or helicopter. It must be able to fire fully automatic for combat in enemy trench systems or built-up areas. Yet the modern combat rifle must be sufficiently accurate to hit enemy soldiers at up to about 440yds (400m) — the longest distance that aimed fire has tended to occur in modern war.

Ammunition must be powerful enough to kill or disable, yet controllable on fully automatic and not so heavy that soldiers cannot carry enough for their mission.

The many mutually-conflicting requirements of military rifles have led different gunmakers to come up with an extraordinary variety of solutions. But before examining the latest ideas for military rifles, it is important to explain how and why the modern "assault rifle" developed as it did.

A hundred years ago, the oldest rifles included in this book were the latest word in military technology. Magazine-loading bolt-action weapons firing (by modern standards) very powerful cartridges, these were capable of accurate fire at over 1100yds (1000m) in the hands of a well-trained soldier. Just as the Iraqi Army was hopelessly trounced by western weapons technology in 1991, so the first Islamic state of modern times — Sudan — was defeated in an equally one-sided battle in 1898. Instead of Stealth bombers and "smart" missiles, the British used Lee-Metford rifles; the Sudanese had spears.

The devastating effect of magazine-loading rifles against closely packed targets was demonstrated again in 1914. German troops armed with the Gewehr 98 (see page 24) inflicted heavy casualties on French infantry who persisted in regarding the bayonet as the most important feature of their Lebel rifle (see page 20). However, the Germans suffered in turn when they encountered British troops equipped with the magnificent SMLE (Short Magazine Lee-Enfield) rifle (see page 32).

The British soldiers were long-service volunteers, trained to a far higher standard than French or German conscripts. Firing 15 aimed rounds a minute — more when badly pressed — this unique army defended its positions with such a hail of fire that the Germans were convinced they faced a line of machine guns. (Ironically, the reason the British Army had devoted so much training time to rapid rifle fire was the government's refusal to buy all the machine guns the Army requested.)

After two years' fighting in World War I it was clear that the existing infantry weapons were no longer suitable for a battlefield

Above: *A French infantryman armed with a Lebel rifle, a design which set the trend for the world's armies of the time.*

Right: *American G.I.s carrying M1 rifles climb the banks of the Rhine during the Allied push into Germany in 1945.*

dominated by artillery and machine-guns. There were no massed targets 1000yds (914m) away: instead, infantrymen found themselves fighting at close-quarters. Hand grenades became a key weapon and the first sub-machine guns were soon in service.

Semi-automatic rifles had already appeared; gun designers in several countries had developed them by the end of the 19th century, but none had entered military service by 1914. Some soldiers viewed them with suspicion, arguing that such weapons would simply lead to excessive ammunition expenditure. Since troops with bolt-action rifles rifles could already fire off all the ammunition they carried in less than ten minutes, what was the point of shooting any faster? On the other hand, some soldiers wanted fully automatic rifles — a number of British officers came to this conclusion as a result of their experiences during the Boer War. It was appreciated that attacking troops needed to lay down suppressive fire on the defenders' positions in order to make a successful assault.

Semi-automatic rifles were used during World War I in limited numbers. Some German aircrew used Mexican Mondragon rifles — made in Switzerland — in the first aerial battles. In 1917 the French introduced several semi-automatic rifles made at the St Etienne arsenal. They were not very reliable, but it was a start. In the USA, J. D. Pedersen developed his "Pedersen device" which fitted into a slightly modified Springfield rifle (see pages 70-71). When inserted, the device allowed the rifle to fire a pistol cartridge instead of its .30" round. At long range, soldiers fired standard ammunition; but for close quarter battle, they were supposed to stop, put this device into their rifles, add a magazine containing 40 modified .32" auto cartridges and continue fighting with what was now a very long sub-machine gun! Some 65,000 of these were made — in conditions of great secrecy — but it was never a practical proposition.

Work on semi-automatic weapons continued after 1918 and in 1936 the US Army became the first to adopt a semi-automatic as its standard service rifle. Designated the M1, it was named after its designer John C. Garand and gave US infantrymen a useful edge

over conventionally-armed opponents (see pages 74-75). It was a superb battle rifle, accurate, hard-hitting and reliable.

By World War II a typical 8-10 man infantry section often included three, different weapons: bolt-action rifles, sub-machine guns and a light machine gun. The soldiers had to carry two, or sometimes three, different kinds of ammunition that were not interchangeable. An obvious answer to this problem would be a weapon that combined the long range accuracy of a rifle with the short range firepower of the SMG. Several gun designers produced rifles capable of fully automatic, but with a few exceptions, like the superb Tokarev M1938, such rifles were uncontrollable.

The main problem was the ammunition. Rifles still fired cartridges developed at the end of the 19th century for long range shooting. To inflict lethal injury at over 1100yds (1000m), rifle bullets needed to be heavy and had to be fired at high velocity. To fire such ammunition on full automatic demanded a heavy gun, usually on a bipod, if the burst was to have a hope of striking the target.

Only the unique German *Fallschirmjägergewehr 42* (see page 24) achieved the theoretically impossible dream: a fully automatic rifle capable of firing the 7.92 x 57mm cartridge. Designed by Louis Strange expressly for the German airborne forces, it was an ingenious response to the paratroops' request for a long range automatic rifle. The German paratroops had suffered catastrophic losses on Crete when, armed with pistols and SMGs, they had had to face British and Commonwealth soldiers shooting SMLEs and Bren guns. To solve the mutually incompatible requirements of such a design, the FG42 sacrificed structural safety and its very efficient muzzle brake produced a vivid flash with every shot. However, the FG42 was an inspiration to post-war weapons design, influencing the British EM-1 and EM-2, which led to the Individual Weapon (see pages 46-47), and the US M60 machine gun.

While the US Army was buying Garand rifles during the 1930s, the Germans were experimenting with lighter cartridges designed for combat at the new battlefield ranges of 330-550yds (300-500m). By reducing the power of the cartridge, selective fire was a realistic possibility and soldiers could carry larger quantities of ammunition. The new cartridge, the 7.92 x 33mm *kurz*, contained half as much propellant as the 7.92 x 57mm. Sacrificing long range performance, the *kurz* round was sufficiently hard hitting and a major step forward.

Assault Rifles

Although the .276″ cartridge developed in the USA anticipated the principal characteristics of the German round, the Germans were the first to introduce a weapon recognizable as a modern assault rifle. The MP44 (see pages 28-29) was introduced despite Hitler's express orders to the contrary and soon proved its value on the Eastern Front. By comparison with modern assault rifles, it is heavy and awkward to fire from prone — but it could still hold its own.

After 1945 most armies accepted the need for a selective fire rifle chambered for a cartridge with similar performance to the 7.92 x 33 *kurz*. In the USSR, Mikhail Kalashnikov had all but completed work on what has become the most widely manufactured combat rifle of all time. His AK47 (see pages 62-63) remains the yardstick for modern combat rifles. Its combination of simplicity and unsurpassed reliability have yet to be matched. While Eugene

Above: *A German paratrooper defends the ruins of the monastery at Monte Cassino in 1944 during the Allied campaign in Italy. The weapon used is the fully automatic Fallschirmjägergewehr 42. Note the Maschinenpistole MP40, or Schmeisser, to his right.*

Right: *Muslim militiamen streetfighting among the barricades of Beirut. Their Soviet-made AK47 assault rifles are excellent and find favour with guerrillas around the world who need weaponry which is durable, dependable and easy to maintain.*

Stoner's superlative AR-15 (see pages 80-81) has demonstratively superior accuracy, the brute strength and dependability of the Kalashnikov makes it the ideal combat weapon for guerrilla forces and Third World armies. No other assault rifle can match the AK's performance in desert or Arctic conditions.

The AK47 was the first in a family of weapons; its successors, the AKM and AK74, have improved upon the original but retained a design continuity and hence a user-friendly continuity too. In the case of the latter there has been a move, just as in the west, to a lighter cartridge of 5.45mm.

As mentioned, in the west there has been — due to NATO standardisation requirements — a drift towards a common calibre of 5.56mm. The pace-setter was the American Eugene

Stoner's M16, now in its third decade of service and updated to M16A2 standard. Other western European countries followed suit and in recent years the Pacific basin countries of the Far East have emerged as weapons designer's and manufacturers. The liberalisation of eastern Europe now offers a further challenge to western arms makers. Israel too is a significant player, her versatile Galil design has been shown to work in combat and numbers among the most successful innovations of the period.

Lightness (available through increased use of plastics) and portability are now crucial design components. The French introduced their FA MAS in the late 1970s and have sold it to several of their former colonies. As it was tested in Chad against Libyan-backed insurgents, it is thought to have performed to expectations in the Gulf War. A more successful weapon in sales terms is Steyr-Mannlicher AG's AUG which is in service with some 20 countries. Of lightweight construction, it is a modular system with built-in sights which offers good value to buyers.

Korea, Singapore, Taiwan and China (adept at copying designs appearing on the market) will all test pricing levels of the most competitive western arms companies but quality, performance and

reliability are the most important factors for the armies which use them and this may work against them.

Military rifles that sacrifice reliability for match-grade accuracy do not endear themselves to the soldiers who have to use them on the battlefield. The infamous British SA80/L85A1 (see pages 46-47) is formidable on a target range, but far too fragile for a service weapon. Its performance in the Gulf War was not encouraging and the few units that can choose their own weapons — the SAS and SBS — will have nothing to do with it.

The US armed forces have devoted considerable energy to developing a successor to the current M16A2 rifle. Heckler and Koch, Colt, Steyr and AAI provided prototypes for an exhaustive series of tests designed to simulate combat conditions as closely as possible. The question was whether anyone could produce a rifle that would deliver a 100 per cent improvement over the M16's battlefield performance. However, despite a wealth of technological solutions — cartridges firing two bullets or steel darts, caseless ammunition, optical sights and many others — the M16 is hard to beat. None of the weapons tested over the last three years seems likely to displace Stoner's design as the ultimate western battle rifle.

Above: *The F88 is Australia's licence-built 5.56mm Steyr AUG. Designed as a convertible weapon (Army Universal Gun), it contains a lot of plastic — note the transparent magazine.*

Left: *Three of the US Army's modern service weapons: the M16A1 fitted with a M203 grenade launcher (left), M16A2 (right), and M249 or Squad Automatic Weapon (centre).*

Right: *French Foreign Legionnaires on a gruelling route march. The leading man carries a 5.56mm FA MAS rifle while his colleague behind has a 7.62mm FR-F2 sniping rifle.*

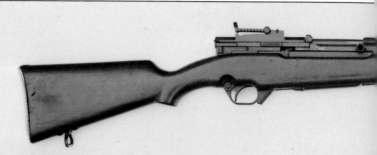

Belgium
SELF-LOADING EXPERIMENTAL MODEL
Development of the SLEM, parent of the FN FAL (below), began in
Belgium in the 1930s and continued in Britain after World War II.

Belgium
FN FAL RIFLE
An early version of the Fusil Automatique Légère; unusual in that
it is made to fire the ·280in round of the British EM 2 rifle.

This arm is one of the 1,000 Belgian self-loaders purchased for
trials by Britain after the abandonment of the EM 2. Battle-tested
in Kenya, Malaya and elsewhere, it was then made in Britain.

SELF-LOADING EXPERIMENTAL MODEL	
Length:	44" (1117mm)
Weight:	9·5lb (4·31kg)
Barrel:	23·25" (591mm)
Calibre:	7·92mm
Rifling:	4 groove r/hand
Operation:	Gas
Feed:	10-round box
Muz Vel:	2400 f/s (730 m/s)
Sights:	1094 yds (1000m)

FN FAL RIFLE	
Length:	41·5" (1054mm)
Weight:	9·5lb (4·31kg)
Barrel:	21" (533mm)
Calibre:	7·62mm
Rifling:	4 groove r/hand
Operation:	Gas
Feed:	20-round box
Muz Vel:	2800 f/s (853 m/s)
Sights:	656 yds (600m)

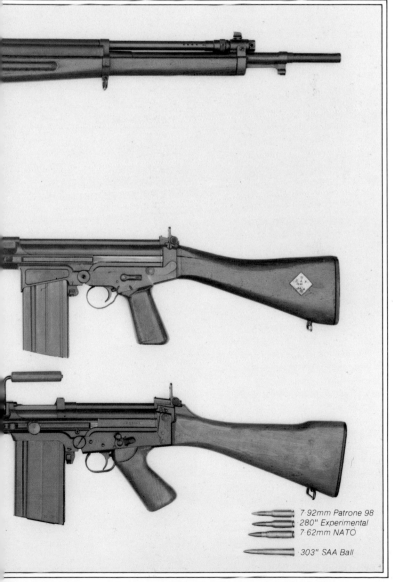

7·92mm Patrone 98
·280" Experimental
7·62mm NATO

·303" SAA Ball

Belgium
SELF-LOADING EXPERIMENTAL MODEL

This weapon was originally designed in Belgium in the 1930s by a M. Saive, who envisaged it as a replacement for the existing bolt-action rifles of Mauser type then in use in the Belgian Army. In May 1940, however, soon after the outbreak of World War II the Germans invaded Belgium and all work on the new rifle naturally stopped. The designer managed to escape from Belgium with the plans for his new weapon which he took with him to Britain.

Saive, like other refugees, continued to work for Great Britain on various wartime projects but nothing was done about his own rifle until the end of the war when a number were made at the Royal Small Arms Factory at Enfield, being generally known as the Self-Loading Experimental Model, often abbreviated to SLEM. They were gas operated with a gas cylinder above the barrel, and had a bolt very similar to that of the Russian Tokarev rifle. They were in general well made and full-stocked in walnut which made them very expensive weapons to produce. These prototypes, which were all made to fire the full size German 7·92mm Mauser round, were extensively tested, but although they proved to be most successful the British were then also carrying out tests on their own EM 2, and so they took no further action on the Belgian rifle. When M. Saive returned to Belgium, however, he continued his work there and soon perfected an improved model known usually as the Model 49, after the date of its appearance. This was a time when a good many countries were looking for cheap and reliable self-loaders with which to re-arm their infantry, and the Model 49 was an immediate success, being sold to a considerable number of countries including Columbia, Venezuela, Egypt and Luxemburg. The Belgians, understandably anxious for business, were more than ready to produce what their customers wanted and the Model 49 was manufactured in a variety of calibres. The Belgian Army also adopted it and it saw service in Korea. It subsequently developed into the highly successful FAL.

Belgium
FN FAL RIFLE

The Belgians, who have long been well known as arms makers, had made considerable progress in developing a self-loading rifle before the war. The designer escaped to Britain with the plans for this weapon which was later made in England and which subsequently formed the basis of all future Belgian

development. Full details of this early weapon are given at the top of this page. The FAL (Fusil Automatique Légère) first appeared in 1950; it was originally intended to fire the German intermediate round, but was subsequently altered to fire the standard NATO cartridge, after which it very soon became popular. It was gas-operated, could fire automatic or single shots as required, and was generally a robust and effective arm well suited to military needs, and sold to a great many countries. Although it had the capacity to fire bursts this led to problems of accuracy due to the inevitable tendency of the muzzle to rise, and most countries therefore had their rifles permanently set at semi-automatic which still allowed twenty or thirty well-aimed shots to be fired in one minute. There was also a heavy barrelled version with a light bipod which some countries adopted as a section automatic. There have been many modifications in design to suit the particular needs of different purchasers, but most of these are relatively minor ones. When Great Britain abandoned her EM 2 she decided, like many other countries, to adopt a version of the Belgian self-loader and purchased one thousand of them for trials, the lower weapon illustrated being one of these originals. As usual some modifications were incorporated and the weapon was fairly extensively tested under operational conditions in Kenya, Malaya, and elsewhere before being taken into use, after which it was made in England. The upper of the two rifles illustrated is a very early version of the Fusil Automatique Légère rifle made to fire the .280" round originally designed for the British EM2 rifle. The object of this is not known, but presumably if the British rifle had been accepted some countries might have preferred a more orthodox looking weapon but in the same calibre as the British EM 2.

NATO troops on the firing line with FN FAL rifles. This Belgian arm first appeared in 1950 and was adopted by over 70 countries.

MODEL VZ 52

Length:	40" (1016mm)
Weight:	9lb (4·08kg)
Barrel:	20·5" (521mm)
Calibre:	7·62mm
Rifling:	4 groove r/hand
Operation:	Gas
Feed:	10-round box
Muz Vel:	2440 f/s (740 m/s)
Sights:	984 yds (900m)

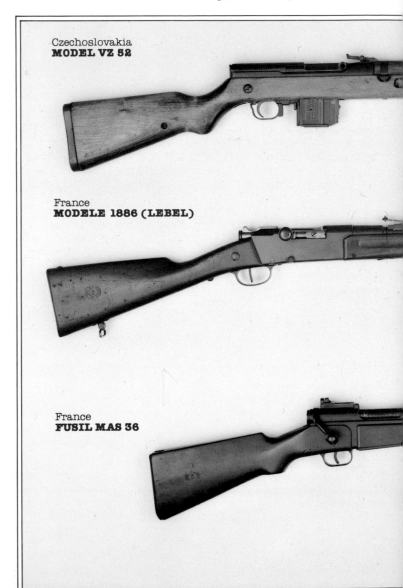

Czechoslovakia
MODEL VZ 52

France
MODELE 1886 (LEBEL)

France
FUSIL MAS 36

MODELE 1886 (LEBEL)

Length:	51" (1295mm)
Weight:	9·3lb (4·22kg)
Barrel:	31·5" (800mm)
Calibre:	8mm
Rifling:	4 groove l/hand
Operation:	Bolt
Feed:	8-round tubular
Muz Vel:	2350 f/s (716 m/s)
Sights:	2187 yds (2000m)

FUSIL MAS 36

Length:	40·15" (1020mm)
Weight:	8·31 (3·76kg)
Barrel:	22·6" (574mm)
Calibre:	7·5mm
Rifling:	4 groove l/hand
Operation:	Bolt
Feed:	5-round box
Muz Vel:	2700 f/s (823 m/s)
Sights:	1312 yds (1200m)

This SLR was developed before the establishment of the Communist regime in Czechoslovakia and later modified — for the worse — at Soviet insistence. The bayonet folds back to the right.

Named for Lt-Col Nicholas Lebel, its chief advocate on the French Small Arms Committee, the Modele 1886 has a tubular magazine which is concealed in the woodwork below the barrel.

The cruciform bayonet of the MAS 36 is carried in a tube beneath the barrel and fixed by plugging its end into the tube.

7·62mm Soviet M43
8mm Mle 86
7·5 Mle 29
·303" SAA Ball

Czechoslovakia
MODEL VZ 52

This self-loading rifle was designed and adopted towards the end of World War II. It incorporated several unusual features. Gas operated it had no cylinder or piston, transmitting power instead by means of a sleeve round the barrel which was forced sharply to the rear by gas pressure and took the bolt with it. The bolt worked on the tilting principle under which the front end of the bolt dropped into a recess cut into the bottom of the body, thus locking it firmly at the instant of firing. It was heavy, which reduced recoil, but also lacked any simple system of gas regulation. It worked well with the intermediate cartridge designed for it, but the imposition of a standard Russian round after the war proved detrimental.

France
MODELE 1886 (LEBEL)

This bolt-action rifle was based on the Austrian Kropatschek which the French Marine Infantry had been equipped with in 1878. It became known as the Lebel after the officer on the French Small Arms Committee who was chiefly responsible for its introduction. It had a tubular magazine in the woodwork below the barrel, the contents of which could be kept as a reserve by using a cut-off device to allow the rifle to be used as a single loader. Rounds were pushed nose first into the magazine opening below the chamber until the capacity of eight had been reached. Its most important feature was the smokeless propellant used in the cartridges instead of the old black powder. This meant that

the firing line could be concealed and the target was not obscured by smoke. The cartridges themselves were bottle shaped instead of cylindrical, enabling them to hold more propellant and thus increasing their power.

France
FUSIL MAS 36

By 1918 automatic weapons dominated the battlefield and the Lebel round's advantages of shape now worked against it. In 1924 a new rimless cartridge was developed, based on the German 7.92mm round, and a new rifle was put into production. The bolt-action MAS 36 was of modified Mauser type but with the bolt designed to lock into the top of the body behind the magazine, making it necessary to angle the bolt lever forward so as to

Left: A French paratrooper at the landing zone at Suez in 1956 is armed with a MAS 36.

be in reach of the firer's hand. The magazine was a five-round integral box and there was no safety catch. Small numbers of a modified MAS 36 were later made for airborne troops; they had shorter barrels and folding butts and were designated the MAS 36 CR39.

France
5.56mm FA MAS

Accepted as its standard rifle by the French Army in the late 1970s this distinctive weapon, with its large carrying handle, is nicknamed Clarion ("Bugle") by soldiers and has proved itself highly effective in general and special forces' service. A compact design, it fires from the closed-bolt position by means of delayed blow-back. Because of its bullpup configuration, the trigger mechanism and pistol grip have been mounted to the fixed, plastic, lower handguard, forward of the magazine well. The grip is ergonomically designed and has a storage trap containing a bottle of lubricant. The sheet metal trigger guard can be pulled away from the rear retaining pin and rotated for firing with gloves under adverse conditions. It has optional right- or left-side ejection and a three-round burst mode as well as single shot or fully automatic. It can be fired from either shoulder or bipod and has an effective range of 300m. Muzzle attachments permit the firing of anti-tank and anti-personnel grenades. There are versions with handle-integrated scopes and there is a shortened barrel version which is intended for use by special forces.

Left: A member of the elite Légion étrangère with his FA MAS on a training exercise.

GEWEHR 98

Length:	49·25" (1250mm)
Weight:	9lb (4·1kg)
Barrel:	29·25" (740mm)
Calibre:	7·92mm
Rifling:	4 groove r/hand
Operation:	Bolt
Feed:	5-round box
Muz Vel:	2850 f/s (870 m/s)
Sights:	2188 yds (2000m)

Germany
GEWEHR 98

Germany
GEWEHR 41(W)

Germany
FALLSCHIRMJÄGERGEWEHR 42

Intended as a specialist weapon for paratroopers, the FG 42 was one of the first assault rifles to see service, from 1942 onwards.

GEWEHR 41(W)	
Length:	44·5" (1130mm)
Weight:	11lb (4·98kg)
Barrel:	21·5" (546mm)
Calibre:	7·92mm
Rifling:	4 groove r/hand
Operation:	Gas
Feed:	10-round box
Muz Vel:	2550 f/s (776 m/s)
Sights:	1313 yds (1200m)

FALLSCHIRM-JÄGERGEWEHR 42	
Length:	37" (940mm)
Weight:	9·95lb (4·5kg)
Barrel:	20" (508mm)
Calibre:	7·92mm Patrone 98
Rifling:	4 groove r/hand
Operation:	Gas
Feed:	20-round box
Muz Vel:	2500 f/s (762 m/s)
Sights:	1313 yds (1200m)

Although its straight bolt lever did not facilitate fast firing,
the Mauser Gewehr 98 served the German Army well in World War I.
Originally made with a five-round magazine, the weapon seen here
has the 20-round box magazine developed in 1918.

Although heavy and somewhat clumsy, this gas-operated self-loader
developed by the famous Walther company proved fairly effective
on the East Front during World War II, until it was superseded
by the Maschinenpistole MP 43/44.

7·92mm Patrone 98
7·92mm Patrone 98
7·92mm Patrone 98

·303" SAA Ball

Germany
GEWEHR 98

The Germans were the first nation to adopt a bolt action rifle which they did as early as 1848 when their needle-gun officially came into service. Thereafter, unlike the British who went off at a tangent with hinged and falling block rifles, the Germans remained constant to this original system which they developed progressively. The first rifle to fire a smokeless round was introduced in 1888 and was of 7·92mm calibre: this was followed in 1898 by the model illustrated which was made by the well-known firm of Mauser. It was a strong and reliable arm with the forward locking lugs made famous by the makers, and a five-round magazine the bottom of which was flush with the stock, and although its straight bolt lever was clumsy and not well adapted to fast fire, this was a minor disadvantage which did nothing to detract from its popularity. In one form or another it was sold to a great number of different countries and there can have been few rifles produced in such large quantities. A considerable number of the earliest ones were bought by the Boers who used them with tremendous effect in their war with the British which broke out a year later, and it served the German Army well in World War I. In 1918 the Germans experimented with a twenty-round magazine to prevent the constant entry of mud from the continuous reloading inseparable from the five-round magazine, but this was not a success chiefly because a spring powerful enough to lift such a column of cartridges made manual operation difficult.

Germany
GEWEHR 41(W)

The Germans were among the pioneers of self-loading rifles and had a complete regiment armed with weapons of this type as early as 1901. This experiment was not followed up, principally because although valuable information was obtained the rifle then used was too heavy for an individual weapon. A few weapons of this type were used in World War I, but the main pre-occupation in 1914-18 was with a great volume of fire from somewhat heavier automatic weapons so again no progress was made. It was not therefore until the appearance of the Russian Tokarev self-loader just before World War II that any real attention was paid to the subject and by 1941 two separate models were undergoing tests. The first was the 41 (Mauser) which incorporated a bolt similar to that of the manually operated rifle; it was never a success and was soon abandoned. The second was the 41 (Walther) and this was a good deal more successful. It incorporated a muzzle cap which deflected part of the gases back onto an annular piston that worked a rod placed above the barrel, its return spring however being below it. This piston rod worked the bolt and the concept was reasonably satisfactory, although the arm had certain defects notably its weight and balance, together with a serious tendency to foul very badly round the muzzle cap. It was manufactured in some quantity and issued chiefly to units on the Russian front. It was eventually replaced by the MP 43/44, a much superior weapon.

A German soldier armed with a 7·92mm Gewehr 98 rifle seeks cover during action.

German soldier with Gewehr 41 rifle slung guards Polish PoWs taken in the fighting of 1939.

Germany
FALLSCHIRM-JÄGERGEWEHR 42

This was one of the earliest assault rifles, being introduced in 1942. Its main disadvantage was that although the Germans had gained some success with intermediate cartridges, this particular arm fired the full-sized rifle round which was really too powerful for it. In spite of this it proved to be a remarkably good weapon to the limited number of troops armed with it, most of whom were parachutists. It was capable of single rounds or bursts. When bursts were employed the FG 42 fired from an open bolt, that is, there was no round in the chamber until the bolt drove one in and fired it in the same movement; the reason for this was that the chamber tended to get sufficiently hot to fire a cartridge left in it even for a very short time. It would take a bayonet and was equipped with a light bipod. Unfortunately it was expensive to make and being something of a specialist weapon for paratroops, its use declined during the war.

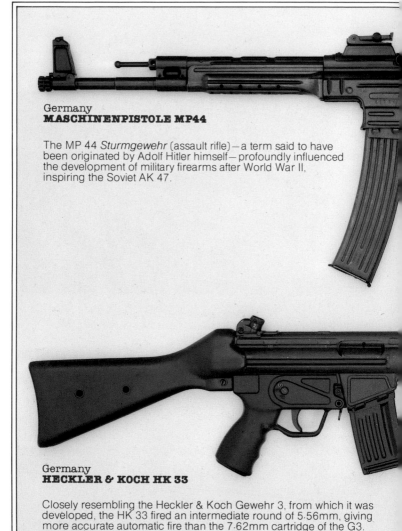

Germany
MASCHINENPISTOLE MP44

The MP 44 *Sturmgewehr* (assault rifle) — a term said to have
been originated by Adolf Hitler himself — profoundly influenced
the development of military firearms after World War II,
inspiring the Soviet AK 47.

Germany
HECKLER & KOCH HK 33

Closely resembling the Heckler & Koch Gewehr 3, from which it was
developed, the HK 33 fired an intermediate round of 5·56mm, giving
more accurate automatic fire than the 7·62mm cartridge of the G3.

MASCHINENPISTOLE MP44

Length:	37" (940mm)
Weight:	11·25lb (5·1kg)
Barrel:	16·5" (420mm)
Calibre:	7·92mm
Rifling:	4 groove r/hand
Feed:	30-round box
Muz Vel:	2125 f/s (647 m/s)
C. Rate:	500 rpm
Sights:	875 yds (800m)

HECKLER & KOCH HK 33

Length:	37" (940mm)
Weight:	7·7lb (3·5kg)
Barrel:	15" (382mm)
Calibre:	5·56mm
Rifling:	6 groove r/hand
Feed:	20-, 30-, 40-round box
Muz Vel:	3145 f/s (960 m/s)
C. Rate:	600 rpm
Sights:	437·5 yds (400m)

7·92mm Kurz
5·56mm × 45mm
·303" SAA Ball

Germany
MASCHINENPISTOLE MP44

The experience of World War I led the Germans to the opinion that in the future the infantryman should have a lighter weapon than the standard rifle. Work on this project started before the war and by 1941 they had produced an efficient intermediate round suitable for a weapon of the kind proposed. Perhaps surprisingly this round does not seem to have been considered for the FG 42, which was being developed at that time but which fired the standard rifle round. Instead a number of weapons were developed for it, and by 1942 these had been whittled down to two, one by Haenel, the other by Walther, both being described as machine carbines. The Haenel version was modified by Schmeisser in 1943 in the light of actual combat experience, after which it became the MP 43, the Walther alternative being dropped at the same time. The new weapon, which was gas operated through a piston working in a gas cylinder above the barrel, was an immediate success and by the end of 1943 the German Army had received fourteen thousand of them. The long-term idea seems to have been to make the MP 43 a universal weapon at squad or section level, so doing away with rifles, sub-machine guns and light machine guns in favour of the new arm. Perhaps fortunately, production declined very rapidly after the first few months of 1944 and so the new concept was never realized. There were some variations to the standard type, notably an MP 43 (1) which

had a fixture allowing it to fire grenades, but no really significant changes. In 1944 the designation was changed to MP 44, apparently to mark the change in year since no other reason was ever offered, and by the end of the same year the weapon had been given the additional title of Sturm-Gewehr, or Assault Rifle. It is said that the expression was coined by Hitler himself; whether this is true or not it was a very apt description and one which has been used ever since. The MP 44 had a profound effect on the development of infantry firearms; the Russians in particular were quick to see the advantages of this new type of arm, and very soon developed their own version in the shape of the AK 47.

Germany
HECKLER & KOCH HK 33

This weapon has a long and somewhat involved history. It had its origins in a German rifle designed in the course of World War II. After the war this rifle was largely redesigned by a number of German designers

and engineers who were working in Spain, the resulting weapon being the Spanish CETME. When the German Army was reformed in the 1950s the German firm of Heckler-Koch, which had been involved with the CETME, developed the design somewhat further and produced a rifle known as the Gewehr 3. This soon became the weapon of the German Army and is, or has been, extensively used by a considerable number of other countries, some of whom bought them from Heckler-Koch while others made them themselves under licence. The G3 was of somewhat unusual design in that it worked not on gas (by far the most common method) but on delayed blowback. The breech was never fully locked in the strict sense of the word; it was equipped with rollers which the forward movement of the firing pin forced outwards into recesses in the receiver. The shape of these recesses and their relationship to the rollers was such that the breech was

held closed until the pressure dropped to a safe level when the rollers were forced out of the recesses. The residual gas pressure in the chamber blew the empty case backwards, taking the bolt with it and compressing the return spring which caused the cycle to be repeated. This method proved to be successful although the use of a full-sized rifle cartridge does often cause problems in a breech of this nature. The main difficulty is that the bolt comes back fairly fast, with no preliminary turning motion to start the case, and this can cause problems of extraction; this was basically the problem of the American Pedersen rifle which is dealt with elsewhere in this section. In the G3 the problem was dealt with by fluting the chamber and by ensuring that the quality of brass used in the case was sufficient to withstand the initial jerk without having its base torn off. The HK 33 was simply a logical development of this earlier weapon, to which it bears a strong resemblance both externally and mechanically. The chief, and important difference is that the HK 33 was designed to fire an intermediate round which offered some advantages. It gave good performance at reasonable ranges and allowed for much more accurate automatic fire than was ever the case with the more powerful 7·62mm cartridge.

The HK 33 is no longer made but there are several derivations from it, including some with telescopic butts, a sniper model, and a shortened version.

German Maschinenpistole MP44 fitted with Krummlauf attachment. With the aid of a periscope, the user was able to fire at angles of 30-90°.

Great Britain
SHORT MAGAZINE LEE-ENFIELD MARKS III AND V

Great Britain
PATTERN 1913 RIFLE

SHORT MAGAZINE LEE-ENFIELD MARKS III AND V		PATTERN 1913 RIFLE	
Length:	44·5" (1130mm)	**Length:**	46·3" (1176m)
Weight:	8·2lb (3·71kg)	**Weight:**	8·7lb (3·94kg)
Barrel:	25" (635mm)	**Barrel:**	26" (661mm)
Calibre:	·303"	**Calibre:**	·276"
Rifling:	5 groove l/hand	**Rifling:**	5 groove l/hand
Operation:	Bolt	**Operation:**	Bolt
Feed:	10-round box	**Feed:**	5-round box
Muz Vel:	2440 f/s (738 m/s)	**Muz Vel:**	2785 f/s (843 m/s)
Sights:	2000 yds (1829m)	**Sights:**	1900 yds (1738m)

Upper: The SMLE Mark III, with its 18in (457mm) sword bayonet, equipped the British Army during World War I.

Lower: The SMLE Mark V, which first appeared in 1923, differs from the Mark III principally in having an aperture backsight in place of the open U-type sight of earlier Lee-Enfields.

Advocates of the forward-locking Mauser system were largely responsible for the development of the Pattern 1913 rifle: a disastrous design — slow to fire, noisy, and prone to excessive fouling in the barrel and over-heating at the breech.

·303" SAA Ball
·303" SAA Ball
·276" Experimental
·303" SAA Ball

Men of the 1st Cameron Highlanders, armed with Short Magazine Lee-Enfield rifles (apparently Mark IIIs) at Cuinchy, April 1918.

Great Britain
SHORT MAGAZINE LEE-ENFIELD MARKS III AND V

British experience in the South African war of 1899-1902 showed the need for a short rifle for universal use and even before the end of the war a new weapon had been produced and a thousand made for trials. It was also tested operationally in the fighting against the Mad Mullah in Somaliland, and after some modification emerged as the Short Magazine Lee-Enfield Mark II in 1907. It was an excellent weapon and although slightly less accurate than its predecessor it had certain compensating advantages, notably its easy breech mechanism which allowed a fast rate of manipulation. The British Army had concentrated on rapid rifle fire to the stage where every soldier could fire at least fifteen well-aimed shots in a minute, and the devastating effects of this were clearly seen in the first few months of World War I when the gallant German infantry suffered heavily. The Mark III was a complex weapon to make, and in 1916 various simplifications were introduced, notably the abolition of the magazine cut-off and the disappearance of the special long-range collective fire sight which was clearly unnecessary in the age of the machine gun. These changed its designation to the Mark III*, perhaps the most famous rifle in British military history. It remained an excellent weapon with an eighteen inch sword bayonet for close quarter work and the ability to project grenades, either rodded or from a screw-on cup. Soon after the end of the war the British began to consider a new rifle, similar to its predecessor but easier to make by modern mass-production methods. The first step in this direction resulted in a new Mark V rifle which appeared in small numbers as early as 1923. Apart from an extra barrel band near the muzzle its main difference was that it had an aperture backsight rather than the open U-type of the earlier rifles, experience having shown that this type of sight was easier to teach, while the increased distance between backsight and foresight reduced the margin of error and made for more accurate shooting. In the end, however, it was decided that the conversion of the large existing stocks of rifles would be too expensive and although the development of a new rifle was maintained the British Army continued to rely on its well-tried Lee-Enfield until well after the outbreak of war in 1939. No separate data is given for the Mark V because apart from the fact that it was only sighted to 1400 yards it differed little from its predecessor.

Great Britain
PATTERN 1913 RIFLE

Although the Lee-Enfield series of rifle had proved remarkably successful there was still some residual prejudice against its bolt in favour of the forward locking Mauser sytem, and this seems to have been the main reason for the development of this new rifle. Work started on it in 1910 and by 1912 it was in limited production for troop trials which began the next year, hence the designation of the arm. Although of unmistakeable Enfield parentage it differed from the earlier range in that it had a Mauser-type bolt and fired a rimless cartridge from an integral five-round magazine. It also had an aperture backsight protected by a somewhat bulky extension on the body above the bolt way. It is perhaps not unfair to describe the Pattern 1913 as a near disaster, for although it

was very accurate there was little else to say for it. It was slow and clumsy to manipulate, particularly for men accustomed to the Lee-Enfield; it was subject to excessive metallic fouling in the bore; it had a tremendous flash and a correspondingly loud report; worst of all, the breech heated so fast that after fifteen rounds or so there was a distinct risk of the round firing as it went into the chamber, which was not conducive to good morale. Although extensive modifications were at once put in hand the project was finally shelved as far as the British Army was concerned by the outbreak of World War I which in view of the major role played by the British rifle in 1914 was probably just as well. Soon after the war started the rifle was converted to fire the standard British service round, but as there were no suitable facilities for making it in the United Kingdom arrangements were made to have it manufactured in the United States by the Winchester, Eddystone, and Remington factories. This new rifle was then designated the Pattern 1914 and in view of its accuracy it was eventually used as a sniping rifle with the addition of a telescope sight. Apart from its different calibre its main external difference from its predecessor was in the absence of the inclined finger slots cut in the stock at the point of balance. The Pattern 1914 was also modified for use by the United States Army, by whom it was designated the Enfield 1917; large numbers of these were bought by Great Britain in 1940, mainly for the use of her Home Guard and the fact that they were of ·30" calibre led to some confusion.

ROSS RIFLE MARK II

Length:	50·5″ (1283mm)
Weight:	9·87lb (4·48kg)
Barrel:	30·15″ (765mm)
Calibre:	·303″
Rifling:	4 groove l/hand
Operation:	Straight Pull
Feed:	5-round box
Muz Vel:	2600 f/s (794 m/s)
Sights:	1200 yds (1098m)

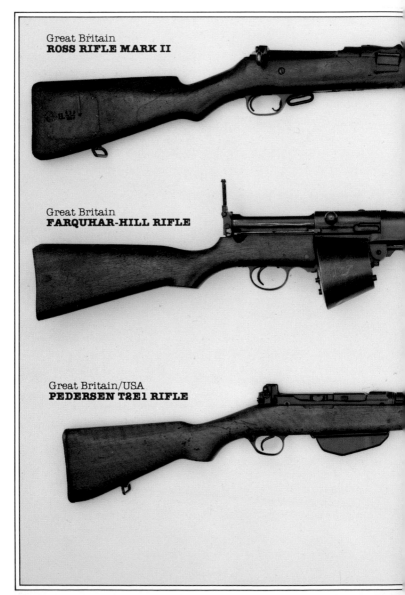

Great Britain
ROSS RIFLE MARK II

Great Britain
FARQUHAR-HILL RIFLE

Great Britain/USA
PEDERSEN T2E1 RIFLE

FARQUHAR-HILL RIFLE		PEDERSEN T2E1 RIFLE	
Length:	41" (1042mm)	**Length:**	45" (1143mm)
Weight:	14·5lb (6·58kg)	**Weight:**	9lb (4·1kg)
Barrel:	27" (686mm)	**Barrel:**	24" (610mm)
Calibre:	·303"	**Calibre:**	·276"
Rifling:	5 groove l/hand	**Rifling:**	6 groove r/hand
Feed:	20-round drum	**Operation:**	Blowback
C. Rate:	6/700 rpm	**Feed:**	10-round box
Muz Vel:	2400 f/s (732 m/s)	**Muz Vel:**	2500 f/s (762 m/s)
Sights:	1500 yds (1372m)	**Sights:**	1200 yds (1098m)

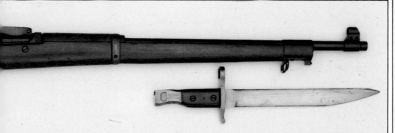

This "straight-pull" rifle was issued to the Canadian Army in 1914, but soon proved to be unsatisfactory.

The third version of an automatic rifle designed before World War I. Note clockwork-powered magazine.

A British committee reported favourably on this rifle in 1932, but cartridge problems prevented adoption.

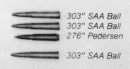

·303" SAA Ball
·303" SAA Ball
·276" Pedersen
·303" SAA Ball

Great Britain
ROSS RIFLE MARK II

This rifle was designed by a Canadian, Sir Charles Ross, towards the end of the 19th Century, first issues being made in 1905 to the Royal Canadian Mounted Police. The rifle was unusual in being of the 'straight-pull' type in which the bolt handle was drawn straight back, the breech being unlocked by the rotation of the locking lugs by means of cams. It had a magazine capacity of five rounds which in the early models had to be loaded singly, and it proved to be an excellent target rifle. There were, however, fundamental defects in its design which rendered it unsuitable as a service rifle and although a whole series of modifications were hastily made there was no significant improvement. The British School of Musketry reported unfavourably on it but in spite of this the Canadian Army went to war with it in 1914, their particular weapon being the Mark III which could be loaded by charger. Its main fault, that the bolt stop bore on one of the locking lugs causing it to burr, led to disastrous consequences, particularly in the mud of the trenches when Canadian soldiers were seen angrily kicking their rifle bolts to open them during German attacks. It was quickly replaced by the Lee-Enfield and little more was heard of it although a few were resurrected for the British Home Guard in the early years of World War II.

Great Britain
FARQUHAR-HILL RIFLE

In 1908 a Major M. G. Farquhar produced an automatic rifle which he had invented in conjunction with Mr. Hill. There was at that time some military interest in automatic rifles and the weapon was tested by the Automatic Rifle Committee which the British Army had set up for the express purpose of investigating weapons of this type. The Farquhar-Hill, although well made by the Beardmore Company, turned out to be an extremely complex weapon. It utilized the system of long recoil, but faulty design kept the barrel and breech locked together long after the bullet had left the muzzle; this and other complications led to problems of feed and the gun was rejected. Nothing more was heard of it until 1917 when a second version appeared; this was described, very accurately, as a light machine gun with some potential as an aircraft gun, but was in fact an improved version of the earlier gun; its main difference was in its unusual magazine which was in the shape of a truncated cone, motive power being provided by a clockwork spring. This version was also tested and rejected, being very liable to fouling and prone to a variety of complex stoppages. It was in any case somewhat late, since it appeared at a time when the Lewis gun was giving good service. The inventors were extremely persistent and as late as 1924 they submitted the weapon illustrated. This had a similar but much smaller magazine with a capacity of ten rounds (as compared with up to sixty-five in the earlier versions) but again it was unsatisfactory (still mainly because of its defective magazine) and was not therefore adopted. Thus it passed into history.

Great Britain/USA
PEDERSEN T2E1 RIFLE

John Pedersen was a well-known designer of firearms in the United States, one of his best known inventions being a device to convert the standard Springfield rifle into a sub-machine gun in 1918. Between the wars he designed a self-loading rifle, together with a special cartridge for it, which attracted favourable attention in America. This new weapon also came to the notice of Messrs Vickers who manufactured a number under licence in England. The Pedersen was unusual in that its breech was not positively locked at the moment of discharge. Instead it made use of a hesitation-type lock, similar in principle to that of the Luger pistol but so designed that its various bearing surfaces held it closed until the chamber pressure had dropped to a safe level. The rifle was tested by the British Government in 1932 and it was described as being the most promising arm of its type that the Small Arms Committee had then seen. In spite of a magazine capacity of only ten rounds it was reported to have fired 140 rounds in three minutes, a remarkable performance. Unfortunately however the breech, although safe, began to open when the chamber pressure was still quite high. This led to difficulties of extraction and in order to overcome this Pedersen had his cartridges dry waxed. This, reasonably enough, was not acceptable in a military cartridge which would have to be stored world-wide in a variety of conditions and climates, so the Pedersen was not finally accepted after all. This was a pity because it was a neat, handy weapon which shot well and its cartridge was of exceptionally good performance. It is possible that it might have performed well with a fluted breech, which was later designed for this type of contingency, but by that time better self-loading rifles were available. It could fairly be argued that this weapon should be listed under the United States. As however the model illustrated was made in England for test by the British Government for possible use by the British Army it seems reasonable to include it under British weapons.

Great Britain
NUMBER 4 AND NUMBER 5 RIFLES

Great Britain
L1A1 RIFLE

A modified FN, the L1 was the standard rifle of the British Army but has now largely been replaced by the Individual Weapon. Note the Trilux night sight.

NUMBER 4 AND NUMBER 5 RIFLES		L1A1 RIFLE	
Length:	44·5" (1130mm)	**Length:**	44·5" (1130mm)
Weight:	9·1lb (4·12kg)	**Weight:**	9·5lb (4·31kg)
Barrel:	25·2" (640mm)	**Barrel:**	31" (533mm)
Calibre:	·303"	**Calibre:**	7·62mm
Rifling:	5 groove l/hand	**Rifling:**	4 groove r/hand
Operation:	Bolt	**Operation:**	Gas
Feed:	10-round box	**Feed:**	20-round box
Muz Vel:	2440 f/s (743 m/s)	**Muz Vel:**	2800 f/s (854 m/s)
Sights:	1300 yds (1189m)	**Sights:**	600 yds (549m)

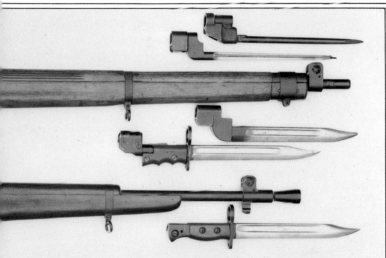

Upper: Seen here with its bayonets, the British Number 4 rifle was mainly produced in Canada and the USA from 1941 onward.

Lower: The shorter Number 5 rifle, designed for jungle fighting.

·303" SAA Ball

·303" SAA Ball

7·62mm NATO

·303" SAA Ball

Great Britain
NUMBER 4 AND NUMBER 5 RIFLES

By 1928 the British Government had developed a new service rifle, similar in general appearance and capacity to the Lee-Enfield but a good deal easier to mass-produce. This new rifle, the Number 4, was a most serviceable arm, its main difference from its predecessor being its aperture sight. It was produced from 1941 onwards, mainly in Canada and the United States, although some were made in England. It underwent some modifications, mainly in the substitution of a simple two-range flip back sight for the earlier and more complex one, and some were made with two-groove rifling, but otherwise remained substantially unchanged, the main feature being perhaps the variety of bayonets made to fit it. Selected specimens were fitted with No 32 telescopic sights and detachable cheek-rests and were successfully used as sniper rifles. It remained in service in the British regular army until 1957,

and some are still used by cadets. It was popular as a target rifle and the current British sniper rifle is based on it. Experience in the Far East showed the need for a shorter weapon for jungle fighting and by 1944 a new Number 5 rifle had been developed. It was closely based on the Number 4 but was five inches shorter and 1·6lb lighter. Its shorter barrel made a flash hider necessary and reduced its muzzle velocity slightly. It was sighted to 800 yards and fitted with a recoil pad to counteract the extra recoil resulting from its reduced weight.

Above: *With a Number 4 rifle slung, General Orde Wingate, creator of the Chindit jungle fighters in Burma during World War II, boards a Dakota (C-47) aircraft. The shorter Number 5 rifle was developed at this time for use in the Far East.*

Above left: *A sniper from a New Zealand unit, armed with a Number 4 rifle, takes up his position in the ruins of Cassino during the Italian campaign of 1944.*

Top: *A rifleman of the 1st Nyasaland Battalion, King's African Rifles, uniformed for jungle warfare — complete with rope for crossing swollen streams — and armed with a Number 5 rifle, in 1952.*

Great Britain
L1A1 RIFLE

This self-loading rifle fires the standard NATO cartridge and will not fire bursts. It is a modified version of the Belgian FN rifle, using glass fibre instead of wood.

It is gas-operated, capable of thirty or forty well-aimed shots a minute, and is generally a sound and reliable weapon. Its principal disadvantage is its length. This was not a problem when Britain had commitments worldwide, but when the Army's role became largely confined to Europe the need was evident for a shorter assault rifle which was more manageable when operating from armoured fighting vehicles and capable of automatic fire in street fighting or other close-quarter work. For this reason the L1A1 is now no longer in general service.

Above: *A British infantryman armed with an L1A1 fitted with a Trilux sight. The rifle has a fold-down cocking handle and is normally a single-shot weapon, but can be made fully automatic by changing the trigger mechanism.*

Left: *A heavily camouflaged soldier using the built-in sights to line-up his target. Effective to over 500m the L1A1 served Britain well for over 20 years and was also built under licence in Canada and Australia.*

Below: *A manually-operated bolt-action single-shot rifle the L4A1 weighs nearly 4.5 kg, has a muzzle velocity of 838 m/s and is fitted with open sights as well as telescopic.*

Great Britain
SNIPER RIFLE L4A1

Sniping first came into large scale use in World War I and World War II soon proved that there was still a need for it. After 1945 the British Army neglected sniping until their long experience in internal security duties around the world made them think differently. Modern self-loading rifles are not well suited to a telescopic sight, so it therefore became necessary to look back rather than forward for a suitable weapon and it so happened that a commercial version of the Number 4 rifle, the Enfield Envoy, was available. It had been developed for target use, cut down to half stock and rebarrelled to fire the standard NATO cartridge. A further number were converted in similar fashion, by the Royal Small Arms Factory, Enfield, and fitted with sights which are a modified version of the original No 32 telescopic sight Although now superseded by the Accuracy International L96A1 some remain in the Army inventory.

SNIPER RIFLE L96A1

Length:	45.78″ (1163mm)
Weight:	13.77lb (6.2kg)
Barrel:	25.78″ (655mm)
Calibre:	7.62mm
Rifling:	4 groove r/hand
Operation:	Bolt
Feed:	10-round box
Muz Vel:	2850 f/s (869 m/s)
Sights:	Telescopic

Great Britain
SNIPER RIFLE L96A1

Great Britain
5.56mm ENFIELD WEAPON SYSTEM

Both Enfield weapons are fitted with robust SUSAT optical sights, but note that the LSW (top) has a longer barrel and a folding bipod.

5.56mm L85A1 INDIVIDUAL WEAPON

Length:	30.9″ (785mm)
Weight:	10.98lb (4.98kg)
Barrel:	20.4″ (518mm)
Calibre:	5.56mm
Rifling:	6 groove r/hand
Feed:	30-round box
Muz Vel:	3084 f/s (940 m/s)
C rate:	650-800 rpm
Sights:	Optical

5.56mm L86A1 LIGHT SUPPORT WEAPON

Length:	35.43″ (900mm)
Weight:	15.17lb (6.88kg)
Barrel:	25.43″ (646mm)
Calibre:	5.56mm
Rifling:	6 groove r/hand
Feed:	30-round box
Muz Vel:	3185 f/s (970 m/s)
C rate:	700-850 rpm
Sights:	Optical

The olive green plastic stock of the Accuracy International sniper rifle is ambidextrous and can be adjusted to suit individual shooters.

Great Britain
SNIPER RIFLE L96A1

Designated Model PM by the manufacturer, Accuracy International, the L96A1 is the British Army's current sniper rifle, issued to Army and Royal Marine snipers. It is available in several versions: the suppressed model has an effective range of 328 yards (300m) using sub-sonic 7.62mm ammunition; the "Super Magnum" version fires .338in Lapua Magnum, .300in Winchester Magnum or 7mm Remington Magnum, all of which offer a significant advantage over 7.62mm ammunition.

The rifle fulfils the needs to put the first shot on target in any environment and for a guaranteed hit at 600 yards (549m), as well as the ability to harass enemy units at up to 1,000 yards (915m). The stock is high-impact plastic and the stainless steel barrel free-floats within it, thus avoiding the distortion sometimes caused when wooden stocks expand and contract. It has an integral bipod and can carry a retractable spike which allows the gun to be set on target and left, without the sniper having to remain in a firing position all the time. The British decision to perservere with a bolt-action rifle may seem outdated but the L96A1 has one which can be operated without the user having to move his head and lose his sight picture.

Great Britain
5.56mm ENFIELD WEAPONS SYSTEM

Britain had adopted the Belgian self-loading rifle because of NATO's rejection of the EM 2 assault rifle designed by the Royal Small Arms Factory at Enfield. By the early 1970s it was clear that an assault rifle would be needed and a smaller, lighter, more mechanically advanced 4.85mm weapon was developed. Although highly effective, it too fell foul of NATO's standard calibre requirements and has thus been further developed, by the now re-named Royal Ordnance

Below: *A sniper pinpoints his quarry with Accuracy International's L96A1 fitted with a Schmidt & Bender 6 x 42 telescopic sight.*

Factories, into the 5.56mm SA 80 or Enfield Weapon System. It is available in two forms, the L85A1 Individual Weapon (IW), or Endeavour, and the L86A1 Light Support Weapon (LSW), or Engager. The IW is a combat rifle of the bullpup type with the magazine located behind the trigger group to make it short, compact and handy. It can be fitted with a bayonet, the

scabbard of which can be used as a wire cutter. The LSW can be regarded as a machine rifle: it is intended to provide longer range support fire for infantry sections and can fire from an open or closed bolt (the IW fires from a closed bolt only). Both weapons have the same general layout and share many common components and mechanisms.

Above: *Two Scottish Fusiliers prepare to enter a building in Belize; the lead man is armed with the L86A1 while his colleague cradles an L85A1.*

Below: *Men of the RAF Regiment guard an airfield during Operation Desert Storm. Note that the airman on the left still carries the L1A1 rifle.*

CEI-RIGOTTI
AUTOMATIC RIFLE

Length:	39·4" (1000mm)
Weight:	9·55lb (4·3kg)
Barrel:	19" (483mm)
Calibre:	6·5mm
Rifling:	4 groove r/hand
Feed:	25-round box
Muz Vel:	2400 f/s (730 m/s)
C. Rate:	Up to 900 rpm
Sights:	1531 yds (1400m)

Italy
CEI-RIGOTTI AUTOMATIC RIFLE

Italy
MANNLICHER-CARCANO CARBINE M1891

Italy
MANNLICHER-CARCANO CARBINE MODEL 1938

MANNLICHER-CARCANO CARBINE M1891		MANNLICHER-CARCANO CARBINE MODEL 1938	
Length:	36·2" (920mm)	**Length:**	40·2" (1022mm)
Weight:	6·6lb (3kg)	**Weight:**	7·6lb (3·45kg)
Barrel:	17·1" (444mm)	**Barrel:**	21" (533mm)
Calibre:	6·5mm	**Calibre:**	6·5mm
Rifling:	4 groove r/hand	**Rifling:**	4 groove r/hand
Operation:	Bolt	**Operation:**	Bolt
Feed:	6-round magazine	**Feed:**	6-round magazine
Muz Vel:	2300 f/s (701 m/s)	**Muz Vel:**	2300 f/s (701 m/s)
Sights:	1640 yds (1500m)	**Sights:**	Fixed 328 yds (300m)

This gas-operated automatic rifle, developed in the 1890s, was tested by the British services early in the 20th century, but rejected for faulty ejection, frequent misfires and inaccuracy.

Although designed for cavalry use this carbine has a folding bayonet, reflecting the realisation that modern warfare would increasingly see cavalry used in a mounted infantry role.

A fixed backsight, set at 300m (328yd), is an unusual feature of this design. An arm of this type, fitted with a telescopic sight, was used in the assassination of President John F. Kennedy.

6·5mm Modello 1891
6·5mm Modello 1891
6·5mm Modello 1895

·303" SAA Ball

Italy
CEI-RIGOTTI
AUTOMATIC RIFLE

Captain Cei-Rigotti, an officer in the Italian Army, appears to have started experiments with gas-operated automatic rifles as early as 1895 when he demonstrated one to his Divisional Commander, the Prince of Naples. Some years were spent in further development thereafter and it was not until 1900 that his efforts were made public in a Roman newspaper, which published a long and laudatory account of his achievements. This included a reference to the use of Mounted Infantry in the war in South Africa, and it was probably this which first drew British attention to the new weapon. Specimens were obtained and a series of tests carried out both by the Small Arms Committee and their Royal Navy counterparts. The rifle worked by a short-stroke piston from the barrel to a rod connected to the bolt, this rod and the cocking handle at its rear end being clearly visible in the photograph, and was designed to fire both single shots and bursts. Although some success was achieved the tests were generally unfavourable, both authorities commenting on the difficulties of ejection and the high rate of misfires, although these may possibly have been due to the fact that the ammunition used had been exposed to seawater on the voyage from Italy. It was also reported that the bolt came so far to the rear in operation that accurate fire was impossible, and some adverse comment was made on the general quality of the workmanship, which was perhaps unfair. It is clear, nearly eighty years later, that the rifle had great potential and many of its features have been copied.

Italy
MANNLICHER-CARCANO
CARBINE M1891

The Model 91 weapons were the first of a series developed for the Italian Army towards the end of the 19th Century. In spite of the inclusion of the word Mannlicher in its official title, it was primarily of Mauser design, the only remaining feature of Mannlicher origin being the six-round clip with which the weapons were loaded and which remained in the magazine until the last round had been fired. They were developed at Turin by S. Carcano, a designer at the Italian Government Arsenal there, and the name of General Parravicino, President of the Italian Small Arms Committee, is often associated with them. The first of the series was a full-

Italian artillerymen armed with Mannlicher-Carcano M1891s: China Relief Expedition, 1900.

length infantry rifle, but this was closely followed by the weapon illustrated, the Model 91 cavalry carbine which actually went into service in 1893. In those days of course, the cavalry still rode horses and therefore needed a short, handy weapon which could be carried either slung across their backs or in a scabbard or bucket on the saddle. The cavalry of most nations at that time were still inclined to delude themselves as to the superiority of the sword and professed to regard fire-arms as of little importance but the pretence was wearing thin. One feature of the Model 91 carbine is its folding bayonet which indicates that even then the Italian cavalry understood that it might have to act as Mounted Infantry and fight on foot. One interesting feature of these early models, which were otherwise undistinguished, was that their rifling was of the type known as progressive twist, i.e. the degree of twist increased progressively towards the muzzle. This was a system originally experimented with by the English inventor, Metford, but soon abandoned as being not worth the increased difficulties of manufacture. The Model 91s were succeeded by a whole series of others, all of similar principle and differing only in detail. These included a model 1938 carbine almost identical with the one illustrated except that it had a fixed backsight. It is illustrated immediately below this entry.

Italy
MANNLICHER-CARCANO CARBINE MODEL 1938

In the course of their Abyssinian campaign of 1936-38 the Italians were somewhat disconcerted to find that their 6·5mm cartridge lacked stopping power. In 1938 therefore they provisionally introduced a 7·35mm round and developed a modified version of their earlier Model 91 to fire it. This new project was however short-lived because when the Italians entered the war in 1940 they were naturally reluctant to embark at the same time on a major change of calibre, so they reverted to their 6·5mm round. There are thus two versions of the Model 1938 carbine, which except for calibre are virtually indistinguishable, the one illustrated being an example of the later reversion to the small calibre. One of its unusual features was the abandonment of the tangent backsight in favour of a fixed one, set at 300 metres. This model 1938 carbine is of considerable interest as being of the type used to assassinate President Kennedy in November, 1963. The particular weapon was an item of Italian war surplus, fitted with a cheap Japanese telescope and purchased by mail order for a few dollars, and it seems to have been an odd choice. The Carcano has no great reputation for accuracy and although its bolt works smoothly enough, the rate of fire must have been slowed down by the telescope. It is notoriously difficult to shoot rapidly through this type of sight, particularly on a carbine with a good deal of recoil, and there has been speculation as to whether the three shots known to have been fired could have come from a single weapon of this type.

Italy
5.56mm BERETTA AR 70

Israel
5.56mm IMI GALIL

5.56mm BERETTA AR 70

Length:	37.6'' (955mm)
Weight:	9.11lb (4.15kg)
Barrel:	17.7'' (450mm)
Calibre:	5.56mm
Rifling:	4 groove r/hand
Feed:	30-round box
Muz Vel:	3135 f/s (950 m/s)
C. Rate:	650 rpm

5.56mm IMI GALIL

Length:	38.6'' (979mm)
Weight:	8.6lb (3.9kg)
Barrel:	18.1'' (460mm)
Calibre:	5.56mm
Rifling:	6 groove r/hand
Feed:	35-round box
Muz Vel:	3230 f/s (980 m/s)
C. Rate:	650 rpm

The folding-butt SC version of the Beretta AR 70 has a fairly traditional rifle layout, takes a bayonet but cannot fire grenades.

Developed by Yakov Lior and Israel Galili the battle-proven Galil assault rifle is produced by Israel Military Industries.

Italy
5.56mm BERETTA AR 70

In the late 1960s Beretta began work on updating the Italian Army's 7.62mm BM 59. They evaluated the leading rifles of the time, hoping to blend their best features with their own innovations to produce a world-beater. Their design appeared in 1970, giving the weapon its name — the Beretta Model 70. The weapon is gas operated but carries no gas regulator. The gas port is placed close to the muzzle end of the barrel, requiring a long piston which is also above it. This raises the centre of gravity of the weapon and, with the magazine below it, the balance and handling characteristics are enhanced. The bolt is forward-locking and the trigger system is simple and clean. The rifle is easily stripped and is available in three versions: the principal type is the assault rifle AR 70 with its high-impact rigid plastic stock with steel butt plate; the Special Troops Carbine or SC 70 is the folding stock version; and the third is a shortened SC 70. The rifle is favoured by Italian special forces and Air Force.

Israel
5.56mm IMI GALIL

This assault rifle — based primarily on the Soviet Kalashnikov — was first issued in 1973 and now has a rich battle-tested heritage. It was noticed in Israel that if the receiver of the Finnish Valmet M62 was used with a stout barrel the system would serve for both 5.56mm and 7.62mm rounds. Each of the three forms of Galil is therefore available in 5.56mm and 7.62mm versions. The rifle has a rotating bolt gas system and, with the exception of the stamped steel breech cover, is fully machined. The wooden foregrip is lined with Dural and has ample clearance around the barrel for heat dissipation. The three forms are: the assault rifle, fitted with a folding metal stock; the short assault rifle with a shortened barrel; and the assault rifle/light machine gun which has a bipod, carrying handle, and can project a variety of

Below: *Marines from Italy's elite San Marco Battalion armed with AR 70s head for their rendezvous point after a beach landing exercise.*

grenades. The trigger and firing mechanisms are those of the M1 Garand, AK series and others. The normal 5.56mm magazine contains 35 rounds, that of the 7.62mm only 25; there is, however, also a 50-round magazine for use as a light machine gun.

The sights give aimed fire out to 500m. A unique and particularly impressive feature is the set of folding night sights which use tritium for illumination; for close quarter work at night — perhaps on border patrols — these sights are undetectable. The Galil was

Above: *An Israeli Naval Commando steals ashore on a training mission perfecting the techniques of infiltration which have been put to good effect on previous occasions.*

adopted by South Africa after the incorporation of modifications such as a carbon plastic stock instead of steel tubing. There it is known as the R4 (Rifle 4) and has proved itself in service with the South African Defence Force in harsh combat terrain in Angola and South West Africa against the combined forces of FAPLA/Cuba and SWAPO.

**MEIJI CARBINE
38th YEAR TYPE**

Length:	34·2" (868mm)
Weight:	7·3lb (3·3kg)
Barrel:	19·2" (487mm)
Calibre:	6·5mm
Rifling:	4 groove r/hand
Operation:	Bolt
Feed:	5-round magazine
Muz Vel:	2400 f/s (732 m/s)
Sights:	2188 yds (2000m)

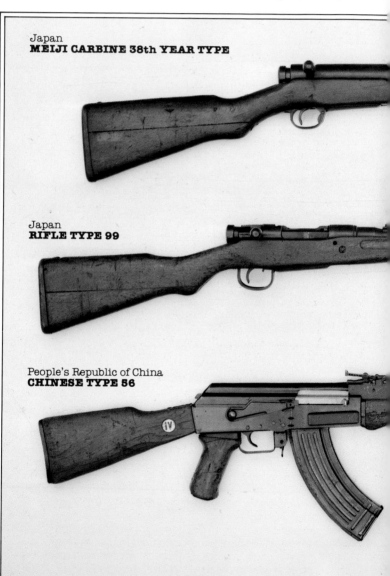

Japan
MEIJI CARBINE 38th YEAR TYPE

Japan
RIFLE TYPE 99

People's Republic of China
CHINESE TYPE 56

RIFLE TYPE 99		CHINESE TYPE 56	
Length:	44" (1117mm)	**Length:**	34·65" (880mm)
Weight:	8·6lb (3·90kg)	**Weight:**	9·45lb (4·3kg)
Barrel:	25·75" (655mm)	**Barrel:**	16·34" (415mm)
Calibre:	7·7mm	**Calibre:**	7·62mm intermediate
Rifling:	4 groove r/hand	**Rifling:**	4 groove r/hand
Operation:	Bolt	**Feed:**	30-round box
Feed:	5-round box	**Muz Vel:**	2350 f/s (717 m/s)
Muz Vel:	2350 f/s (715 m/s)	**C. Rate:**	600 rpm
Sights:	2625 yds (2400m)	**Sights:**	875 yds (800m)

This carbine is a shortened version of the rifle of the same designation, which had a service life from 1905 into World War II. Note the metal dust cover over the bolt.

The "short" version of the rifle adopted by Japan before World War II: the "normal" version was some 6in (152mm) longer. Note the folding wire monopod—a refinement of dubious value.

A close copy of the Soviet AK 47, the Chinese-made Type 56 assault rifle differs from its parent principally in having a permanently-attached folding bayonet of cruciform section.

7·7mm Type 99
7·62mm Soviet M43

·303" SAA Ball

Japan
MEIJI CARBINE 38th YEAR TYPE

Japan made a remarkable change from a medieval to a modern state in the second half of the 19th Century. Her first rifle was a single shot bolt action model of 11mm calibre which appeared in 1887 but which was replaced almost immediately by a rifle of smaller 8mm calibre with a tube magazine. Her war with China in 1894 showed some defects in her armament and a commission headed by Colonel Arisaka was appointed to investigate the whole matter and make recommendations for improvement. The result was a series of Mauser type rifles, first adopted in 1897 and often known as Arisaka rifles. Their alternative title was the Meiji 30th year type, having been made in the 30th year of the rule of Emperor Meiji. Rifles of this type were used in the war against Russia in 1904-5 and a number were purchased by the British in 1914 to train their new Armies. The 38th year type came into use in 1905 and was an improved version of the earlier model. It had a long life, being used in World War II. The 38th year carbine was simply a shortened version of the rifle for use by arms other than infantry, and would take the standard bayonet. It had a metal dust cover over its bolt, similar to the one on the British Lee-Metford, but it proved very noisy in close-quarter jungle fighting. In many ways it would have been a better service weapon for the infantry than the long rifle, being much handier. Like most carbines however it suffered from fairly heavy recoil. There was a 1944 version with folding bayonet.

Japan
RIFLE TYPE 99

Japanese experience in China in the 1930s (like that of the Italians in the same period) showed the need for a more powerful cartridge than the 6 5mm they then used, and

A US observer of the Russo-Japanese War took this photograph of a Japanese infantryman taking aim with his Meiji 30th Year Type rifle. The 38th Year Type of 1905 was an improved version.

after a good deal of experiment they settled in 1939 for a rifle built to fire a rimless version of their 7·7mm round already used in their 1932 model medium machine gun. The original intention of the Japanese had been to use a carbine, which would have been a good deal handier type of weapon in view of the small size of most of their soldiers. Carbines however, particularly when firing powerful rounds, inevitably have increased recoil, which would adversely affect any lightweight soldiers, however tough and hardy they might be. As a compromise the new rifle, which was designated the Type 99, was made in two lengths, a 'short' rifle in line with modern European custom, and a 'normal' version some six inches longer, the one illustrated being of the shorter type. This new rifle had a rather odd attachment in the shape of a folding wire monopod which was designed to support the rifle when fired from the prone position, but although of some theoretical advantage it can have been of little practical value due to its lack of rigidity. The backsight was also fitted with two graduated horizontal extensions to right and left, intended to be used to give a degree of lead when firing at crossing aircraft; nothing is known regarding their effectiveness. The Type 99 was not widely used in World War II.

People's Republic of China
CHINESE TYPE 56

The Chinese fought their war against the United Nations in Korea with a considerable mixture of outdated weapons mainly of American, Russian, or British origin, but after it was over the Russians started arming their fellow Communists with a variety of more up to date Russian arms notably the SKS carbine, the AK 47 assault rifle, and the RPD light machine gun, all of which fired the same 7·62mm intermediate cartridge. The demand however was enormous and as soon as they were able to do so the Chinese set up their own factories to manufacture military weapons. As there was considerable urgency over the matter, the Chinese wasted no time in trying to produce new or original designs, but simply stuck as closely to the originals as their own somewhat less sophisticated manufacturing techniques allowed them. The weapon which they originally concentrated on was a locally developed version of the SKS, but this now seems to have been relegated to a training role in favour of their Type 56 assault rifle. Mechanically this is a very close copy of the original AK 47, the principal difference being a permanently attached folding bayonet of cruciform section. Although this is a very old idea, the Chinese are by·now the only country still using it, all others having opted for a detachable knife-type bayonet which the soldier can use as a general purpose implement, which is what most modern bayonets are now used for.

Chinese-made Type 56 rifles were extensively used in Vietnam by the Viet Cong who found them to be ideal weapons for soldiers who were mostly small and slight by Western standards; the specimen illustrated is one of the many captured there by the American Army. They are also found in considerable numbers in the Yemen and other Middle East countries and as insurgent weapons in African nations.

Soviet Union

Length:	40" (1016mm)
Weight:	8·9lb (4kg)
Barrel:	20·4" (518mm)
Calibre:	7·62mm
Rifling:	4 groove r/hand
Operation:	Bolt
Feed:	5-round magazine
Muz Vel:	2700 f/s (823 m/s)
Sights:	1093 yds (1000m)

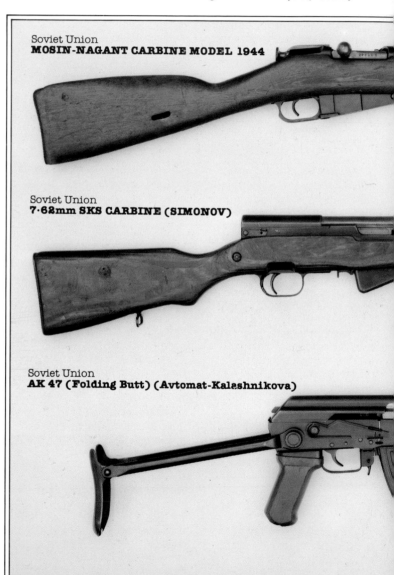

Soviet Union
MOSIN-NAGANT CARBINE MODEL 1944

Soviet Union
7·62mm SKS CARBINE (SIMONOV)

Soviet Union
AK 47 (Folding Butt) (Avtomat-Kaleshnikova)

7·62mm SKS		**AK 47 (Folding Butt)**	
CARBINE (SIMONOV)		**(Avtomat-Kalashnikova)**	
Length:	40·2" (1022mm)	**Length:**	34·65" (880mm)
Weight:	8·5lb (3·86kg)	**Weight:**	9·45lb (4·3kg)
Barrel:	20·5" (521mm)	**Barrel:**	16·34" (415mm)
Calibre:	7·62mm	**Calibre:**	7·62mm
Rifling:	4 groove r/hand	**Rifling:**	4 groove r/hand
Operation:	Gas	**Feed:**	30-round box
Feed:	10-round box	**Muz Vel:**	2350 f/s (717 m/s)
Muz Vel:	2410 f/s (735 m/s)	**C. Rate:**	600 rpm
Sights:	1093 yds (1000m)	**Sights:**	875 yds (800m)

The last in a series of arms that began with a Russo-Belgian design of 1891. Note the permanently-attached bayonet, here seen folded back along the right-hand side of the weapon.

The SKS, an efficient if somewhat bulky self-loading rifle which appeared during World War II, again featured a folding bayonet. Until superseded by the AK 47, it was a favourite guerrilla arm.

The folding metal butt of the AK 47 can be turned forward under the weapon without in any way interfering with its operation.

7·62mm 1891g
7·62mm Soviet M43
7·62mm Soviet M43

·303" SAA Ball

Soviet Union
MOSIN-NAGANT CARBINE MODEL 1944

The first Mosin-Nagant arms were developed by Colonel Sergei Mosin of the Russian Artillery, and a Belgian designer named Nagant. The 1891 model was the first of the modern small-bore bolt-action magazine rifles to be used by Russia and virtually all her later rifles of the type are based on it. The basic rifle was of fairly orthodox design and took a somewhat outmoded socket bayonet. There were several variations, chiefly in the length of the barrel. The calibre was originally measured in an old Russian unit known as a line and equivalent to 1/10" As a result they were often known as 'three-line' rifles until the metric system was introduced after the Revolution. Their sights were also calibrated in arshins, another ancient measurement based on the human pace. Many of these earlier rifles were made in other European countries, and during World War I the United States manufactured one and a half million of them for Russia. The next major change came in 1930, although even this was little more than a general modernization of the early type. It did however lead to the production of a sniper version with a telescopic sight. The weapon illustrated was introduced towards the end of World War II and was the very last of the Mosin-Nagant series to be made. It was still very similar to its predecessors, but incorporated a permanently attached bayonet which folded back along the right side of the rifle when not in use. It had an unpleasant chisel point which can be seen just behind the backsight in the illustration of the carbine .

Soviet Union
7·62mm SKS CARBINE (SIMONOV)

This was an early type of self-loader, developed and produced by Russia in the course of World War II. It was a gas operated weapon of orthodox appearance, and was designed to fire an 'intermediate' round of the type originally developed by the German Army for their MP 43/44. It had a magazine capacity of ten rounds which could be loaded either separately or by clips, and was equipped with a folding bayonet of bladed type, which turned back under the barrel when not required. The woodwork was of laminated beech, heavily varnished. The SKS

Escorted by a guard with a slung SKS (Simonov) carbine, an East German couple are turned back at the Berlin border, 1961. Soldier in foreground is armed with a slung PPSh 41 sub-machine gun.

was an efficient weapon, if somewhat heavy, and the cartridge gave adequate power at the sort of ranges envisaged in modern war, which by Russian techniques were of the order of three or four hundred metres. This was probably a perfectly practical maximum for an Army well equipped with machine guns of one kind or another. The SKS was used and manufactured by many Communist bloc countries, and a number of non-communist states, among them Egypt, were equipped with it. At one period it became very much a standard guerrilla arm, being widely used in Aden, the Yemen, Oman and elsewhere in the Middle East, but by now it has

been largely superseded by the ubiquitous AK 47 in its various forms, and survives mainly as an arm for watchmen, village home guards, and other relatively humble organizations which do not require advanced firearms.

Soviet Union
AK 47 (Folding Butt) (Avtomat-Kalashnikova)

The earliest versions of the AK 47, which came into use in the Russian Army in 1951, had wooden butts. These, like many other early Soviet arms, were of poor quality timber which detracted greatly from the otherwise excellent quality and finish of the new arms as a whole. Soon afterwards there appeared an alternative version with a folding metal butt which could if required be turned forward under the weapon without affecting its use. This type was probably originally intended for use by airborne troops, but its compactness made it easily concealed and therefore an obvious weapon for guerrillas, terrorists, and similar irregular organizations and it now appears to be almost universally used all over the world in this role. Apart from its compactness the AK 47 has certain other obvious advantages in this respect; it is strongly made and shoots as well as an orthodox rifle to four hundred metres with the additional advantage of automatic fire if needed. Perhaps even more important is its general simplicity; the sort of organizations using it rarely have the time or facilities for extensive training of recruits so that something which can be taught quickly to an individual with no previous experience of firearms is useful.

Soviet Union
AK 47

Finland
M62 ASSAULT RIFLE (THE VALMET)

AK 47		M62 ASSAULT RIFLE (THE VALMET)	
Length:	34·65" (880mm)	**Length:**	36" (914mm)
Weight:	9·45lb (4·3kg)	**Weight:**	8lb (3·6kg)
Barrel:	16·34" (415mm)	**Barrel:**	16·5" (419mm)
Calibre:	7·62mm intermediate	**Calibre:**	7·62mm
Rifling:	4 groove r/hand	**Rifling:**	4 groove r/hand
Feed:	30-round box	**Feed:**	30-round box
Muz Vel:	2350 f/s (717 m/s)	**Muz Vel:**	2350 f/s (718 m/s)
C. Rate:	600 rpm	**C. Rate:**	650 rpm
Sights:	875 yds (800m)	**Sights:**	875 yds (800m)

Although now supplanted in Soviet service by the AKM assault
rifle, Kalashnikov's AK 47 remains perhaps the most common
military firearm throughout the modern world.

The Finnish Defence Forces' Valmet assault rifle — the latest
version, with minor modifications, is the M76 — makes an
interesting comparison with the mechanically-similar AK 47.

7·62mm Soviet M43
7·62mm M60
·303" SAA Ball

Soviet Union
AK 47

Germany's MP 44 assault rifle was the inspiration for Mikhail Kalashnikov's AK 47 design which went into service in 1951. It worked by gas tapped off from the barrel and impinging on a piston working in a cylinder above the barrel. This piston took with it a rotating bolt, the whole being thrust forward again by the coiled return spring at the proper time. It is accurate and shoots well on automatic up to about 300 metres without undue vibration. It is well made and easily stripped. It fires an intermediate 7.62mm cartridge which, contrary to popular belief, is not inter-changeable with the NATO round. The bore is chromed and the weapon takes a bayonet. It has a good claim to being the most common military firearm in the world.

Soviet Union
AKM

The AKM is an improved version of the AK 47. A lighter weapon, it entered service in 1961 and makes extensive use of metal stampings and plastic. It has a cylic-rate reducer, compensator and maintains the high and accurate volumes of fire of its predecessor. It can be fitted with luminous or infra-red sights and a multi-use bayonet. It is available either with a wooden stock or with a folding metal stock designated AKMS.

Soviet Union
AK 74

Developed in 1974 and entering service in about 1977 this is the latest rifle in Soviet service. The folding stock version, AKS 74, was first seen during the Red Square Parade of that year. Basically it is a re-chambered, re-bored AKM firing a 5.45mm cartridge. It is identifiable by some external differences: a distinctive, two-port muzzle brake, which increases its length slightly; horizontal grooves on the foregrip and butt; and a smooth plastic magazine which is slightly shorter and less curved than that of the grooved metal AKM.

Below: *Soviet Naval Infantry on the Black Sea coast. Note the distinctive smooth plastic form and red colouring of the AK 74's magazine.*

The muzzle brake uses a fluidic device to excellent effect in minimising recoil and muzzle climb; however, the gas cylinder is vulnerably placed and may cause malfunctions if dented. It has proved itself a first class weapon in combat in Afghanistan where Spetsnaz tested derivatives such as the AKS-74U, a much shortened version with folding stock.

Finland
M62 (THE VALMET)

Always closely associated with her more powerful neighbour, Finland developed her first Soviet type assault rifle in the late 1950s. Mechanically it was identical to the AK 47 but with external differences. Made at Valmet, the Model 60 was all-metal, much of it plastic covered. It had a plastic forehand grip ventilated with a series of holes and a rather ugly tubular butt with a

Above: *Known by the Finns as the RK 62 the Model 62 assault rifle is also in service with the ground forces of Qatar.*

shoulder piece welded onto the end. Also it had no trigger guard, merely a vertical bar in front of the trigger. The object was to allow gloved hands to fire it during the fierce Finnish winters, but it must have increased the risk of accidental discharge. The Model 62 makes increased use of pressings and riveting. It has the same curved magazine and a tangent backsight mounted on the receiver cover. The three-pronged flash hider incorporates below it a bayonet bar. From the mid-1980s Model 62s have been given folding stocks and more robust machined steel receivers instead of sheet metal. A further variant, the Model 62/76, was essentially a Finnish AKM but production now centres on the improved Model 62.

KRAG-JORGENSEN CARBINE MODEL 1896

Length:	41.5" (1054mm)
Weight:	7.75lb (3.51kg)
Barrel:	22" (559mm)
Calibre:	30/40"
Rifling:	4 groove r/hand
Operation:	Bolt
Feed:	5-round magazine
Muz Vel:	2000 f/s (610 m/s)
Sights:	2000 yds (1829m)

United States of America
KRAG-JORGENSEN CARBINE MODEL 1896

United States of America
RIFLE MODEL 1895 (US NAVY)

United States of America
US RIFLE MODEL 1903 (SPRINGFIELD)

RIFLE MODEL 1895 (US NAVY)		US RIFLE MODEL 1903 (SPRINGFIELD)	
Length:	47" (1194mm)	**Length:**	43·2" (1097mm)
Weight:	8lb (3·63kg)	**Weight:**	8·7lb (3·94kg)
Barrel:	27·25" (692mm)	**Barrel:**	24" (610mm)
Calibre:	236"	**Calibre:**	·30"
Rifling:	5 groove l/hand	**Rifling:**	4 groove r/hand
Operation:	Straight-pull	**Operation:**	Bolt
Feed:	5-round magazine	**Feed:**	5-round box
Muz Vel:	2400 f/s (732 m/s)	**Muz Vel:**	2800 f/s (813 m/s)
Sights:	2000 yds (1828m)	**Sights:**	2700 yds (2469m)

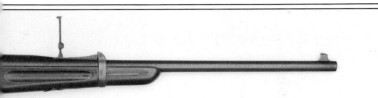

The US Army's first bolt-action, magazine rifle (carbine version seen here), in general issue by 1894, saw service in the Spanish-American War of 1898 and the Philippines Insurrection, 1899-1905.

This rifle, adopted by the US Navy in 1895, is better known as the "Lee straight pull"; a reference to the breech mechanism, which is operated by direct backward pressure on the lever.

Called the Springfield from its place of manufacture, this rifle was in general US issue by 1906, replacing the Krag-Jorgensen.

·30" Model 1898
·236" Model 1895
·30" '06 Springfield

·303" SAA Ball

United States of America
KRAG-JORGENSEN CARBINE MODEL 1896

This was the first bolt-action magazine rifle to be used by the United States Army. It was officially adopted in 1892 to replace the old single-shot Springfield but did not come into general issue until 1894. It was closely based on a weapon invented by Captain Ole Krag of the Danish Army and an engineer named Eric Jorgensen, and the United States paid these inventors one dollar for every one made in America. It was of normal bolt action, its most unusual feature being a five-round box magazine on the right hand side which had to be loaded, one cartridge at a time, through a loading gate which incorporated the magazine spring. The raised thumbpiece by which it was opened is clearly visible in the photograph. There were a number of variations, none of them very important. It was used by the regular Army in Cuba in 1898 although the Militia still had the single-shot Springfield. Soon after the introduction of the Krag-Jorgensen, the United States decided to adopt a new rifle based on the Mauser system and the Krag then disappeared from the military scene. It was an excellent rifle and many converted examples are still in use as sporting rifles in the United States. The specimen illustrated is of interest because it is one of the last carbines used by the United States before the adoption of a standard rifle for general issue regardless of arm or service, which occurred with the introduction of the 1903 Springfield.

The first contingent of the American Expeditionary Force to arrive in England, 1917, parades with Model 1903 (Springfield) rifles and equipment stacked.

United States of America
RIFLE MODEL 1895 (US NAVY)

This rifle is probably better known as the Lee straight-pull which indicates both its inventor and its mechanism. James Lee, a Scot by birth but educated in Canada, eventually became a citizen of the United States where all his experimental work was done. He is probably best known for his box magazine for bolt action rifles; it was widely adopted and his name appears on a long series of British service rifles. Towards the end of the 19th Century he invented a rifle which in 1895 was adopted by the United States Navy who placed an order for ten thousand of them. The rifle was unusual in that it incorporated a 'straight-pull' breech in which direct

Soon after the introduction of the Krag-Jorgensen rifle into the United States Army in 1894 the authorities began to examine the idea of yet another rifle, this time on the Mauser principle, and five thousand infantry models with thirty-inch barrels were ordered in 1901. Before they were made however the United States Army decided that the time had come for a short universal rifle, and had the barrels reduced to twenty-four inches. In this they were probably influenced by their experience in Cuba and also by the lessons of the Anglo-Boer War which caused the British Army to reach a similar conclusion. The new rifle, commonly known as the Springfield after its place of manufacture, had a Mauser type bolt and a five-round magazine with a cut-off, and after some basic modifications, notably the introduction of a lighter, pointed bullet, in place of the earlier round-nosed variety, it was brought into general issue by 1906. It proved to be a very popular rifle, its chief disadvantage, a minor one, being its small magazine capacity, and remained in use for many years. In this time it underwent various modifications, notably one to allow it to be converted to an automatic weapon by the addition of the Pedersen device of 1918 and another which added a pistol grip to the stock in 1929. There was also a target variety, equipped with a Weaver telescopic sight, which was used successfully as a sniping rifle in World War II.

backward pressure on the lever caused the breech to rise slightly, opening as it did so. No manual turning was required, locking worked by an arrangement of cams on the bolt. It was of unusually small calibre and had a magazine capacity of five rounds; it was also the first United States service rifle ever to be loaded by means of a charger. Unfortunately straight pull rifles have no real advantage over the more orthodox turn bolt types, but they do have several disadvantages, chief of which are their complex structure and the fact that their operation, perhaps surprisingly, is more tiring than that of normal types. The United States Navy disliked it very much and it soon disappeared from the service. A sporting version was also made but this also proved unpopular and the model was soon withdrawn, some 18,300 of the 20,000 produced never seeing daylight.

RIFLE ·30 CAL M1 (GARAND)

Length:	43·50" (1103mm)
Weight:	9·50lb (4·37kg)
Barrel:	24" (610mm)
Calibre:	·30"
Rifling:	4 groove r/hand
Operation:	Gas
Feed:	8-round internal box
Muz Vel:	2800 f/s (853 m/s)
Sights:	1200 yds (1097m)

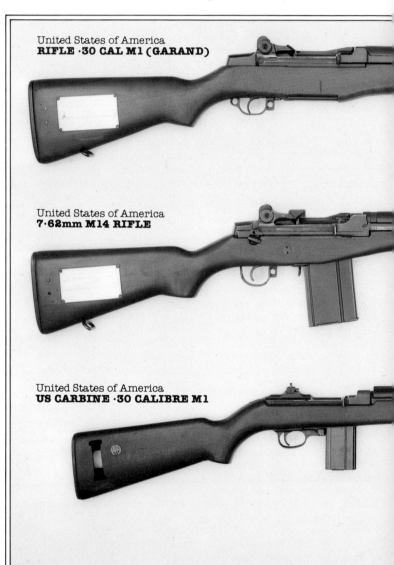

United States of America
RIFLE ·30 CAL M1 (GARAND)

United States of America
7·62mm M14 RIFLE

United States of America
US CARBINE ·30 CALIBRE M1

7·62mm M14 RIFLE	
Length:	44" (1117mm)
Weight:	8·55lb (3·88kg)
Barrel:	22" (558mm)
Calibre:	7·62mm
Rifling:	4 groove r/hand
Feed:	20-round box
Muz Vel:	2800 f/s (853 m/s)
C. Rate:	750 rpm
Sights:	1000 yds (915m)

US CARBINE ·30 CALIBRE M1	
Length:	35·65" (905mm)
Weight:	5·45lb (2·48kg)
Barrel:	18" (458mm)
Calibre:	·30"
Rifling:	4 groove r/hand
Operation:	Gas
Feed:	15/30-round box
Muz Vel:	1950 f/s (585 m/s)
Sights:	Fixed, 300 yds (275m)

The first self-loading rifle adopted as a standard weapon by any army, in 1936, the Garand featured an internal 8-round magazine.

Design of the M14, standard US rifle in the 1950s and 1960s, was based on wartime experience with the Garand. A 20-round pre-fillable box replaced the unsatisfactory clip-loading system.

Although of the same calibre as the Garand, the M1 carbine fired a straight pistol-type cartridge, and was closer in concept to a stocked Mauser or Luger self-loading pistol than a modern SMG.

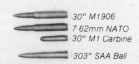

·30" M1906
7·62mm NATO
·30" M1 Carbine
·303" SAA Ball

RIFLE · 30 CAL M1 (GARAND)

This rifle, commonly known as the Garand, was the first self-loader ever to be adopted by any army as a standard weapon. A whole series of similar rifles were exhaustively tested before it was finally selected in 1936. It was a good weapon, very robust (and therefore heavy) but simple and reliable. It was operated by gas and piston. The magazine had a capacity of eight rounds and had to be loaded by a special charger holding that number of cartridges in two staggered rows of four each. When the last round had been fired the empty clip was automatically ejected and the bolt remained open as an indication to the firer that reloading was necessary. The Garand was the standard rifle of the United States Army in World War II, and was the only self-loader generally used. They were made mainly by the Springfield Armoury and the Winchester Repeating Arms Company, although smaller numbers were also produced by other American arms

companies and after the war a quantity were made by the Italian firm of Beretta. When manufacture finally ceased in the middle 1950s an astonishing total of some five and a half million had been produced. There were inevitably a number of variations to the Garand in its long history, including a National Match model and no less than three sniper rifles, but none of them differed from the prototype.

Below: *US soldiers in training charge with bayonets fixed on their M1 (Garand) rifles.*

Above left: *Fording a stream, a soldier of the US Signal Corps holds his M1 carbine at high port.*

Left: *With his battered M1 carbine slung, a USMC Staff-Sgt fraternises with a young internee in the Pacific, 1944.*

United States of America
7·62mm M14 RIFLE

Before the end of World War II the American Military authorities were working on the concept of a selective fire weapon of assault rifle type. By 1953, NATO having settled on a common cartridge, good progress had been made, and although most European countries opted for Belgian type weapons the United States settled for the M14. This was a logical development of the Garand. Based on war experience a number of important improvements had been made, notably the abolition of the awkward eight-round clip and the substitution of a pre-filled detachable box magazine holding twenty rounds. The new rifle was capable of firing single shots or bursts, and although most were issued permanently set for semi-automatic fire only, a number were fitted with light bipods with a view to being used as squad or section light automatics. They were however only marginally suitable for this role because sustained fire caused them to overheat and there was no provision for changing barrels. A heavy barrelled version was at one time contemplated but never produced, and there was also an excellent sniper version. The M14 saw quite extensive use in the Vietnam war. Some 1,500,000 were made in all, but it is no longer manufactured and although United States NATO forces still use it, it is no longer the standard American rifle. As soon as the NATO countries finally settle on a new cartridge it will become obsolete.

United States of America
US CARBINE ·30 CALIBRE M1

The term carbine, like many military words, has meant different things at different periods. By the end of the 19th Century it was generally used to denote a short version of the standard infantry weapon for use by mounted troops, but in the next few years the universal rifle became common in most armies and the term tended to lapse. Just before World

Above: *The soldier on the wrecked tank holds an M1 rifle.*

Top: *US soldier in white camouflage suit, with M1 rifle, guards Belgian clearing, 1944.*

Right: *A US sniper poses with M1 rifle fitted with telescopic sights and flash eliminator.*

War II the United States Army decided that it needed a new light weapon, intermediate between the pistol and the rifle, as a convenient arm for officers and non-commissioned officers at rifle company level and as a secondary weapon for mortarmen, drivers and similar categories for whom the service rifle would have been awkward. The request, originally made when peacetime financial measures were in force, was at first refused but once war seemed

inevitable it was granted and by the end of 1941 the Army had settled for the M1 carbine and it had gone into large scale production. The M1 was a short, light, self-loading rifle, and although its calibre was the same as that of the service rifle it fired a straight pistol-type cartridge, so that there was no question of inter-changeability between the two. The M1 carbine was an odd, indeed an almost unique, weapon to have been produced so late, since in a very real sense it looked back towards the arms of the stocked Luger or Mauser pistol-type, rather than forward to the sub-machine gun, which at the time of the introduction of the new carbine had amply demonstrated that it had an important part to play in modern warfare. At that period the United States sub-machine gun was however still the Thompson, heavy and expensive to produce, and these considerations probably justified the introduction of a new category of arm.

US CARBINE ·30 CALIBRE M1A1

Length:	36·65" (931mm)
Weight:	5·45lb (2·48kg)
Barrel:	18" (458mm)
Calibre:	·30"
Rifling:	4 groove r/hand
Operation:	Gas
Feed:	15/30-round box
Muz Vel:	1950 f/s (595 m/s)
Sights:	Fixed. 300 yds (275m)

United States of America
US CARBINE ·30 CALIBRE M1A1

United States of America
ARMALITE AR-15 (M16)

The lightness and portability of the M16 make it ideal for jungle warfare or for soldiers of small stature. Several millions have been manufactured and the weapon is in worldwide use.

United States of America
COLT COMMANDO

Mechanically similar to the M16, the Colt Commando has a telescopic butt and short barrel to facilitate close-quarter use. Note the removeable 4in (102mm) long flash hider.

ARMALITE AR-15 (M16)

Length:	39" (991mm)
Weight:	6·35lb (2·88kg)
Barrel:	20" (508mm)
Calibre:	233" (5·56mm)
Rifling:	4 groove r/hand
Feed:	30-round magazine
C. Rate:	800 rpm
Muz Vel:	3250 f/s (991 m/s)
Sights:	500 yds (458m)

COLT COMMANDO

Length:	28" (711mm)
Weight:	6·55lb (2·97kg)
Barrel:	10" (254mm)
Calibre:	223" (5·56mm)
Rifling:	4 groove r/hand
Feed:	20/30-round magazine
C. Rate:	750 rpm
Muz Vel:	3000 f/s (915 m/s)
Sights:	500 yds (458m)

Basically the same weapon as the M1 carbine, the M1A1 had a folding stock for use by airborne and parachute forces. The stock's central bracing plate contains an oil bottle.

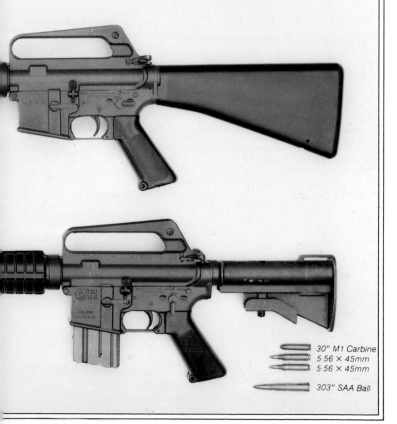

·30" M1 Carbine
5·56 × 45mm
5·56 × 45mm
·303" SAA Ball

United States of America
US CARBINE .30 CALIBRE M1A1

A variation on the M1, the M1A1 had a folding stock pivoted on a pistol grip so that the carbine could be fired if necessary with the stock folded, making it a convenient weapon for airborne forces. The M1 series was produced in enormous numbers and was a light, handy weapon which in spite of some lack of stopping power fulfilled an obvious need. Two further versions were developed: the M2, which was a selective fire version, and the M3, designed to take various types of night sight.

United States of America
ARMALITE AR-15 (M16)

Developed from the AR-10, the small calibre, high velocity AR-15 was designed by Eugene Stoner and made by Colt from 1959 onwards. Light and easy to handle it was adopted by the United States during the Vietnam War, becoming the standard rifle. It has no piston, the gases simply passing through a tube and striking directly onto the bolt. This is efficient but means that the weapon needs careful and regular cleaning because the design makes the weapon sensitive to propellant that leaves too much residue. In

Above: *British paras, one with an M1A1, take cover as intra-Greek fighting erupts in Athens in December 1944.*

Right: *A soldier from the US 82nd Airborne Division carries an M16A2 and takes a radio message during the Gulf War.*

1967 changes were made to the bolt system, creating a forward assist assembly and a new designation, the M16A1. In 1985 the M16A2 was introduced offering a three-round burst facility instead of fully automatic. Experiences in Vietnam had shown that men tended to fire long bursts of automatic fire which after three shots made the muzzle climb and the rest of the shots miss. Accurate and highly reliable, the M16A2 is also lighter than most other 5.56mm weapons. It is popular with British special forces and may be further adapted by the US Army to M16A3 standard. A specialised version, the Colt M231, exists for use from IFV's firing ports.

United States of America
COLT COMMANDO

Mechanically identical to the M16, this weapon has a ten-inch barrel instead of the M16's twenty-inch. The intention was to produce a sub-machine gun with the accuracy and hitting power of an assault rifle. Tested in Vietnam it was found that the reduced muzzle velocity had a

serious effect on longer range accuracy. Heavy muzzle flash also made a hider necessary, but this can be unscrewed and special forces tended to prefer the loud, intimidatory effect. The Commando or CAR-15 has a telescopic butt for use when fired from the shoulder.

Right: *A US Navy SEAL armed with one of the weapons favoured by American elite forces — the Colt Commando.*

The Sub-Machine Gun

A British soldier armed with a 9mm L2A3 Sterling sub-machine gun. Introduced in 1953 this simple and reliable weapon was used until the late-1980s when the 5.56mm SA 80 rifle replaced both it and the L1A1.

The sub-machine gun (SMG) is an automatic weapon which fires pistol cartridges and is light enough to be used two-handed from the shoulder or hip without other support. Such arms were first used to meet an urgent need for close-range firepower in World War I. Italy introduced the Villar-Perosa, a double-barrelled arm firing a 9mm rimless self-loading pistol cartridge, in 1915, but although of obvious utility in trench warfare, it was not as widely adopted as might have been expected.

Next in the field were the Germans, who armed some infantry with stocked self-loading pistols of Luger and Mauser type. These were not true automatic weapons, for the trigger had to be pressed for each shot, but they proved efficient. To avoid too

frequent reloading, magazines with a capacity of 30-plus rounds were produced, and from this it was but a short step to the development of a true SMG (which the Germans designate a machine-pistol).

The MP 18 Bergmann

Hugo Schmeisser produced the MP 18.1, usually known as the Bergman, in time for use in the German offensive of spring 1918, and some 35,000 were made by the summer of that year. Although Germany's defeat obscured the Bergmann's true significance it was, in fact, the prototype for almost all similar weapons thereafter. Thus, a brief description of its operation will serve for all weapons of the type.

The Bergmann had a barrel just under 8in (203mm) long and a heavy, cylindrical bolt with a permanently-attached cocking handle. Its 9mm cartridges were carried in a ''snail drum'' magazine (see page 102). To fire, the bolt was drawn back manually against a spring and was held to the rear by a sear. When the trigger was pressed, the sear was freed and the spring drove forward the bolt, stripping a cartridge from the magazine, forcing it into the chamber, and firing it. No locking device was

Above: *Armed with Stens, battle-weary British paras advance through the ruins during fierce fighting at Arnhem.*

Below: *Soviet Naval Infantry with PPSh 41 SMGs hoist their ensign during the liberation of Sevastapol in May 1944*

Above: French troops open fire on Communist guerrillas across a rice paddy in Indo-China. The soldier exposing himself to enemy fire has a MAT-49 sub-machine gun at his side.

needed: the heavy bolt was still travelling forward as it fired the cartridge, and by the time the rearward thrust of the cartridge halted and reversed this movement, pressure had dropped to a safe level. The cycle repeated as long as there was pressure on the trigger and rounds in the magazine. Cyclic rate of fire was about 400 rpm; there was no provision for single shots. The original sighting, to 1000m (1094yds), was unrealistic: the bullet was probably fairly accurate up to c200m (220yds) but, being fired from a low-powered pistol cartridge, had relatively little stopping power at that range.

American Developments

The Allies' only real attempt to produce a similar weapon was the American Pedersen Device, a small machine-pistol which fitted into the breech of a standard Springfield rifle and fired a magazine of pistol ammunition. It was never used in action.

A much better arm was the SMG developed by Colonel (later Brigadier-General) J.T. Thompson, USA; but the first gun to bear his name did not appear until 1921. The Thompson, popularly associated with gangsters and terrorists, perhaps only became "respectable" on its adoption by the US Army in 1938. With the coming of World War II, hundreds of thousand of Thompsons were made for use by the Allies.

None of the other American SMGs of World War II—including the complex Reising and the functional M3 "grease gun"—achieved the fame of the "tommy gun". It is notable that all American SMGs fired the standard .45in cartridge for the 1911

Above: *Uzi-armed members of the Policia Nacional man a Latin American border post. A dozen or so countries in the region have acquired the gun, either from IMI in Israel or FN in Belgium.*

Colt self-loading pistol: although an excellent cartridge, this was in many ways too powerful, and made the weapons a good deal heavier to handle than was desirable.

Britain's Wartime Need

The period between the two World Wars saw a steady increase in the use of the sub-machine gun, particularly during the Spanish Civil War. Britain tested various models, but when war actually broke out in 1939 was compelled to order a large number of Thompsons. They were reliable but old-fashioned compared with those of the Axis powers, thus Britain began to design and produce indigenous sub-machine guns.

A light, simple, easily manufactured weapon for mass-production was what was wanted. A copy of the MP 28 was produced known as the Lanchester but it was little used; then in 1941 the Sten gun appeared. It was built by the million and went through a series of marks, becoming more and more simplified for ease of manufacture and even running to a special silenced version. Even German ingenuity could not improve on the Sten as a simple arm for mass-production and they copied it for use by the home defence militia known as the *Volkssturm*.

German and Soviet Developments

After 1918 the Treaty of Versailles restricted the German Army's use of automatic weapons. Ways around this were found, however, and by 1922 Germany was again making sub-machine guns — the Steyr-Solothurn — in Switzerland. Within a few years pretences

were abandoned and extensive rearmament began. In 1938 the all-metal, folding stock MP 38 was adopted, more commonly known as the Schmeisser. Although it underwent modifications during the war it remained substantially unchanged.

The Russians do not appear to have developed a successful machine gun until 1934 and the PPD. This was a sound and reliable weapon with a 71-round drum, which made it rather heavy. Like all Soviet arms of this type it fired the bottle-shaped 7.62mm pistol cartridge.

The Russians were the major users of the sub-machine gun in World War II. Having lost much of their industrial capacity early on they found it was much easier to make than more sophisticated weapons and produced them by the million. It proved a successful arm in the desperate close-quarter fighting in the besieged cities and whole regiments were eventually armed with it.

The Decline and Revival of the SMG

The development of the assault rifle at the end of World War II seemed to threaten the whole concept of the sub-machine gun. Soldiers could now be equipped with selective fire rifles that out-performed the SMG on every count. More accurate than the blowback SMGs then available, weapons like the AK 47 or the later AR-15 were harder hitting and just as reliable. The Red Army, which had equipped a high proportion of its infantry with SMGs, withdrew them from frontline service during the 1950s. There were two exceptions to this trend: the embattled state of Israel needed to mass produce its own weapons quickly and Major Uziel Gal came to the rescue with a cheap and simple SMG soon known as the UZI (see pages 98-99); elsewhere, Communist China sent hundreds of thousands of soldiers armed with Soviet-style SMGs to invade Korea.

Some armies remained opposed to issuing fully automatic weapons and adopted semi-automatic rifles instead. The British bought the Belgian FN FAL and modified it to prevent fully automatic fire; the French acquired the MAS 49/56 self loading rifle. Both armies retained a sub-machine gun in each infantry squad — the British selecting the Sterling (see page 126) and the French the robust MAT-49 which gained favour with their elite forces. Even the US Army retained its M3 "Grease guns" as the standard SMG well into the 1970s.

It was the NATO armies' gradual acceptance of 5.56mm rifles that really spelt the end of the SMG as a frontline military weapon. SMGs had always been popular in jungles where the fighting was inevitably at very close range, but the M16 rifle proved an even better bet — first in Borneo, then in Vietnam. Its much more powerful cartridge and far longer reach made it a more versatile weapon altogether. The British Army is phasing out its Sterling SMGs and equipping all soldiers with the SA80. The French have retired the MAT-49 in favour of the FA MAS assault rifle.

Many commentators in the 1970s drew the conclusion that the SMG was finished as a military weapon. However, the SMG does have its advantages in internal security operations and the most famous modern SMG, the Heckler & Koch MP5 (see page 106), is

Left: *Germany's GSG9 practise a hostage rescue; the two body-armoured troopers in the foreground have MP5s fitted with sophisticated telescopic sights and silencers.*

used by most western special warfare units. It is also employed by many US SWAT teams and European paramilitary units; and since the late 1980s they have been issued to the British police at major airports. The MP5 fires from a closed bolt which makes it much more accurate than traditional SMGs like the Sterling. It does, however, require careful maintenance and is therefore not suited to jungle warfare or similar. Available in many different guises, there is even a version chambered for the powerful 10mm cartridge. The value of the relatively short-ranged 9mm round had led the wheel to turn full circle: both the M16 and Steyr AUG assault rifles are now available chambered for 9mm Parabellum! The US Marine Corps anti-terrorist units used their 9mm M16s during the liberation of Panama in 1989. Because the bullets do not travel as far as rifle rounds, the risk of civilian casualties — always high in an insurgency — is substantially reduced.

The sub-machine gun is still therefore very much alive, although in American circles the Ingram is rather out of favour. The Colt Commando is not a true sub-machine gun, rather it is a lightened version of the Armalite, but Sturm Ruger have designed a 9mm MP9 sub-machine gun and it remains to be seen how much this will interest the US Army.

Other countries have continued to develop this field, notably those in Europe. The 7.65mm Skorpion has been produced in Yugoslavia by Zastava and remains an excellent personal protection weapon. The 9mm Finnish Jatimatic has a lot of plastic for lightness and its unusual design succeeds in giving very stable automatic fire. The Italian company Beretta were responsible for the sturdy and compact 9mm PM 12 which is used by their special forces and paramilitary carabinieri. In Poland, the RAK PM-63 is a 9mm, open bolt weapon of simple design which is used by their anti-terrorist squad.

Undoubtedly, the premier European sub-machine gun is the Heckler & Koch. Accurate, easily controlled on automatic, and available in a multiplicity of specialised versions it sets the high standards for others to better. Its popularity has helped to secure the future of the sub-machine gun as a highly useful arm in the face of pressure from the assault rifle.

Left: *Philippino Scout Rangers with Colt Commando SMGs track elusive Communist insurgents on Mindanao Island where an insurgency has raged for decades.*

Below: *An Italian Folgore paratrooper with the Beretta PM 12 which serves a number of other armies and is also licence-built abroad. The weapon is favoured by Italy's elite and special forces units.*

Czechoslovakia
ZK 383

Czechoslovakia
VZ 61 (THE SKORPION)

A true machine pistol, the Skorpion is little larger than an early self-loading pistol. Light and easily concealed, it is particularly well suited to police and security work.

ZK 383

Length:	35·4" (899mm)
Weight:	9·37lb (4·25kg)
Barrel:	12·8" (325mm)
Calibre:	9mm
Rifling:	6 groove r/hand
Feed:	30-round box
C. Rate:	500 and 700 rpm
Muz Vel:	1250 f/s (365 m/s)
Sights:	875 yds (800m)

VZ 61 (THE SKORPION)

Length (f):	10·65" (271mm)
Weight:	2·9lb (1·31kg)
Barrel:	4·5" (114mm)
Calibre:	7·65mm
Rifling:	6 groove r/hand
Feed:	10/20-round box
C. Rate:	700 rpm
Muz Vel:	970 f/s (294 m/s)
Sights:	Flip 82-164 yds

The standard Bulgarian SMG of World War II—also manufactured and used by the Germans—the ZK 383 is unusual in having a folding bipod, which is said to have contributed much to its accuracy.

9mm Parabellum
7·65mm Auto Pistol

·303" SAA Ball

Czechoslovakia
ZK 383

This weapon, which was designed by the Koucky brothers at Brno, first appeared in 1933 and was still in production three years after the end of World War II. It is a most sophisticated and very well made weapon, manufactured of precision castings of excellent finish, and cannot have been cheap to produce. It is of particular interest in having a dual rate of fire; this is achieved by removing a weight on the bolt, which increases its rate of functioning.

There is also a quick release barrel, although it is not clear whether this was for changing in action or simply to facilitate cleaning. The ZK 383 will fire either single rounds or automatic as required, the change lever above the trigger being pushed back or forward as necessary. The stud behind it is the push-in safety. The pierced barrel casing carried the foresight and a well made tangent backsight. Another unusual feature is its folding bipod, which when not required for use is turned backward into a recess in the woodwork. This bipod is said to make a considerable

Above: *Czechoslovakian VZ 61 (Skorpion) sub-machine gun with its light wire butt folded forward. This does not affect the operation of the weapon.*

Inset: *A soldier fires the Skorpion from the shoulder, with butt extended. Note his forward grip on the magazine.*

improvement in the accuracy of the gun, but even so it is likely that the maximum setting of 800 yards is optimistic.

This was the standard sub-machine gun used by the Bulgarian Army during and after World War II. The Germans continued to manufacture it after they had over-run Czechoslovakia and it was used by their SS troops. A modified version was also produced for police use. It had no bipod and no tangent sight. It is believed that there was a variation of the standard gun with a bipod which folded forward. Some models took a bayonet.

VZ 61 (THE SKORPION)

This is a good example of the rather small number of true machine pistols, its general dimensions being comparable to those of the Mauser pistol model 1896. It is therefore of relatively limited use as a military weapon, except possibly for tank crews, motor cyclists and similar categories for whom a compact secondary weapon is more important than performance. Its small calibre also reduces its stopping power although of course the use of automatic fire helps considerably in this respect. There is also a bigger version, made only in limited quantities, which fires a 9mm round and is in consequence a good deal heavier although similar in essence. The Skorpion works on the normal blowback system. Very light automatic weapons often have the disadvantage that their cyclic rate of fire is unacceptably high, but in this weapon the problem is largely overcome by the use of a type of buffer device in the butt. It has a light wire butt for use from the shoulder; this can be folded forward when not required without affecting the working of the weapon. Although the size and capacity of the Skorpion reduces its military efficiency, it is an excellent weapon for police or other forms of internal security work since it is inconspicuous and easily concealed. Its low muzzle velocity also makes it relatively easy to silence, and an effective model is available which is an additional advantage in this sort of role. It has been sold to many African countries.

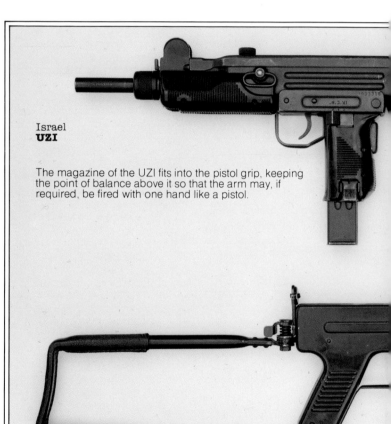

Israel
UZI

The magazine of the UZI fits into the pistol grip, keeping
the point of balance above it so that the arm may, if
required, be fired with one hand like a pistol.

Denmark
MADSEN MODEL 50

Note the unusual grip safety behind the magazine housing. The tubular
metal stock pivots to fold on the right side of the weapon.

UZI

Length:	25.2" (640mm)
Weight:	7.7lb (3.5kg)
Barrel:	10.2" (260mm)
Calibre:	9mm
Rifling:	4 groove r/hand
Feed:	25/32/40-round box
C. Rate:	600 rpm
Muz Vel:	1280 f/s (390 m/s)
Sights:	Flip. 110-219 yds

MADSEN MODEL 50

Length:	31.25" (794mm)
Weight:	6.95lb (3.15kg)
Barrel:	7.8" (199mm)
Calibre:	9mm
Rifling:	4 groove r/hand
Feed:	32-round box
C. Rate:	550 rpm
Muz Vel:	1250 f/s (365 m/s)
Sights:	Fixed

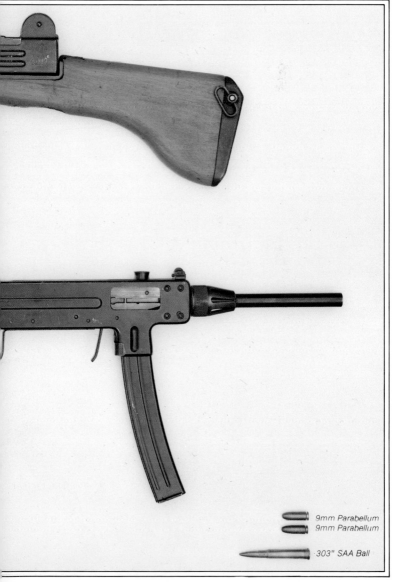

9mm Parabellum
9mm Parabellum

.303" SAA Ball

Israel
UZI

At midnight on 14 May, 1948
the British mandate over
Palestine ceased, and the
Jewish State of Israel was
declared. On the very next day
the new state was invaded by
its Arab neighbours, and there
followed nearly eight months of
war, at the end of which Israel
had not only defended her own
territory successfully but had
also occupied some of that
belonging to her attackers.
In spite of her success
however it was clear that she
needed a reliable weapon
which she could make from
her own resources in sufficient
numbers to arm the bulk of her
population if necessary, and by
1950 Major Uziel Gal of the
Israeli Army had designed the
weapon illustrated. Production
started almost immediately and
still continues to date.
The UZI works on the normal
blowback principle and is made
from heavy pressings in
conjunction with certain heat-
resistant plastics. The rear end
of the barrel extends backward
into the body and the front of
the bolt is hollowed out so as to
wrap round this rear projection.
The magazine fits into the pistol
grip which affords it firm
support and also keeps the
point of balance above it, so
that the gun can if necessary be
fired one-handed like a pistol. It
fires single rounds or bursts as
required. Most of the early UZIs
had a short wooden butt 8
inches long, as illustrated, but a
very few were made longer.
Later models have a folding
metal stock. It is made under
licence in Holland and used by
many other countries.

*An Israeli soldier on the alert
with his 9mm UZI sub-machine gun;
the design dates from 1950.*

The UZI is a most effective arm for street fighting. The model seen here has its folding metal stock fully extended.

Denmark
MADSEN MODEL 50

The first sub-machine gun to be made in Denmark was a type of Finnish Suomi, made under licence by the Danish Madsen Industrial Syndicate in 1940. Production continued throughout the war, the gun being used not only by the Danes themselves but by the Germans and the Finns. The same syndicate has made all Danish sub-machine guns since. The first weapon of the present series was the Model 1946, and the Danes, profiting from wartime advances in mass production, made sure that it was designed in such a way as to be able to take advantage of these improved techniques. The main body, including the pistol grip, is made from two side pieces, hinged together at the rear, so that the weapon can be easily opened for repair, cleaning or inspection. It does, however, have the disadvantage that springs are liable to fall out unless care is taken. The Madsen works on the normal blowback system and will fire single rounds or bursts as required. One of its unusual features is a grip safety behind the magazine housing which (with the magazine itself) acts as a forward hand grip. Unless this safety is in the gun will not function, which makes it impossible to fire it one-handed. The tubular metal stock is on a pivot and folds onto the right side of the weapon. The Model 50, the gun illustrated, is similar to the Model 46, the main difference being the milled knob cocking handle which replaced the flat plate of the earlier model. When the new Model was demonstrated in 1950 many countries showed great interest in it and the delegation from Great Britain was sufficiently impressed to recommend that it should be considered in the search for a new weapon to replace the Sten gun. It was tested against other arms and was recommended for adoption by non-fighting troops if the new British EM 2 rifle made a sub-machine gun unnecessary for the infantry. In the event the new rifle was not adopted and the Sterling was taken into general use. The curved magazine actually belongs to the later model.

Germany
BERGMANN MP18.I

Germany
BERGMANN MP28.II

BERGMANN MP18.I

Length:	32" (813mm)
Weight:	9·2lb (4·18kg)
Barrel:	7·88" (200mm)
Calibre:	9mm
Rifling:	6 groove r/hand
Feed:	32-round snaildrum
C. Rate:	400 rpm
Muz Vel:	1250 f/s (365 m/s)
Sights:	Flip 110-219 yds

BERGMANN MP28.II

Length:	32" (812mm)
Weight:	8·8lb (4kg)
Barrel:	7·8" (199mm)
Calibre:	9mm
Rifling:	6 groove r/hand
Feed:	20/30/50-round box
C. Rate:	500 rpm
Muz Vel:	1250 f/s (365 m/s)
Sights:	1094 yds (1000m)

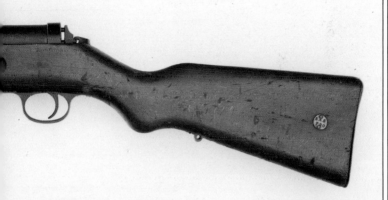

Although it appeared too late to change the course of World War I, this Schmeisser-designed, Bergmann-manufactured arm was, in 1918, the first sub-machine gun to make a significant battle appearance.

Significant changes from the MP18.I (above) include a straight box magazine rather than the complex "snail drum" and ability to fire either bursts or single shots.

9mm Parabellum
9mm Parabellum

·303" SAA Ball

Germany
BERGMANN MP18.1

By the end of 1914 World War I had settled down to a static if bloody business of opposing trenches resembling a two-sided siege on a huge scale and this relatively new type of warfare brought into use a whole host of new weapons; some of these, like mortars and grenades, were simply modernized versions of long obsolete items, but some were genuinely new, and the sub-machine gun comes into this latter category. The first to appear on the actual battlefield was the Italian Villa Perosa of 1915. This was, however, rather complex and in spite of its obvious potential it does not seem to have made any great impression.

The Germans soon began to arm a proportion of their infantry with stocked pistols of the Mauser and Luger type (both of which are dealt with elsewhere in this book), and it was a short step to the introduction of a somewhat heavier version with the capacity to fire bursts. Work on a prototype weapon started in 1916 at the Bergmann factory, the designer being Hugo Schmeisser, the famous son of an almost equally famous father, and by the early months of 1918 it was in limited production. The Germans, always realists, appreciated that at that late stage of the war, when their manufacturing capacity was fully extended, any new weapon would have to be simple to make and the MP 18.I fulfilled that requirement. The techniques of mass production by the use of pressings, spot welding, and pinning were, however, hardly developed so that 'simple' is a relative term when compared with, say, the Sten gun of a quarter of a century later. The Bergmann was machined, and although elaborate milling had necessarily been abandoned, its general finish was relatively good. Its weakest component was its magazine, which was a of a type originally developed for the Luger pistol, and which was too complex and liable to stoppage to be fully reliable. The Germans proposed to have six guns per company; each was to have a number two to carry ammunition, and there were to be three hand carts in addition, which presupposed a type of barrage fire, but it came too late. Its main interest is therefore its influence on future design, which was very significant.

Above: *German soldier advances with his 9mm Bergmann MP28.II sub-machine gun.*

Below left: *German policeman with MP28.II and, apparently, spare magazines of drum type.*

Germany
BERGMANN MP28.II

The MP 18.I issued to the German police for internal security purposes in 1919 had been slightly modified by Schmeisser in the light of practical experience in the previous year. The chief change was a new magazine housing designed to take a straight box magazine of modern type rather than the complex clockwork-operated snail drum which had given a good deal of trouble in the conditions of trench warfare. A few years later the same designer made even more improvements, and as these were sufficient to warrant a new designation the modified MP 18.I appeared in 1928 as the MP 28.II, the II denoting two minor modifications to the prototype. The new gun had some interesting features, chief of which was its ability to fire either bursts or single shots as

required. This was controlled by a circular stud above the trigger, which had to be pushed in from the right for automatic, and from the left for single shots. The gun also incorporated an elaborate tangent backsight graduated by hundreds up to a thousand metres, which must have been far outside any practical service range. It was equipped with straight box magazines, but the magazine housing was so designed that it would if necessary accept the old snail drum type. These various improvements did not change its general appearance very materially so that it still resembled the old MP 18. The Bergmann MP 28.II was produced in Germany by the Haenel Weapon Factory at Suhl, but as there were still some restrictions on domestic production of military firearms a great many more were produced under Schmeisser licence by a Belgian company in Herstal, and it was adopted by the Belgian army in small numbers in 1934. The Bergmann soon established a reputation for reliability and was purchased in South America (where it was extensively used in a series of small wars there) and by the Portuguese who used it as a police weapon. Although it was mainly manufactured in 9mm Parabellum, it also appeared in 9mm Bergmann, 7·65mm Parabellum, 7·63mm, and even for the American ·45" cartridge. It seems probable that its main use was in the Spanish Civil War of 1936-39, where its robust construction made it an ideal weapon for the militias by whom the war was mainly fought. It ceased to be made before World War II, but had a revival in the shape of the British Lanchester.

Germany
MASCHINENPISTOLE MP40 (SCHMEISSER)

Germany
HECKLER & KOCH MP5 A5

One of the truly great weapons in use today, Heckler & Koch's
MP5 A5 sub-machine gun is the three-round burst version of the
earlier MP5 A3.

MASCHINENPISTOLE MP40 (SCHMEISSER)		HECKLER & KOCH MP5 A5	
Length:	32.8″ (833mm)	**Length:**	19.3″ (490mm)
Weight:	8.87lb (4kg)	**Weight:**	6.3lb (2.9kg)
Barrel:	9.9″ (251mm)	**Barrel:**	9″ (225mm)
Calibre:	9mm	**Calibre:**	9mm
Rifling:	6 groove r/hand	**Rifling:**	6 groove r/hand
Feed:	32-round box	**Feed:**	15/30-round box
C. Rate:	500 rpm	**C. Rate:**	800 rpm
Muz Vel:	1250 f/s (365 m/s)	**Muz Vel:**	1320 f/s (400 m/s)
Sights:	Flip. 110/219 yds	**Sights:**	Adjustable

One of the most famous weapons of World War II; more than one million had been made by 1945. Schmeisser, its manufacturer, probably had no part in its design.

Germany
MASCHINENPISTOLE MP40
(SCHMEISSER)

In spite of the success of the Bergmann in the closing months of World War I, it was not until 1938 and the lessons of the Spanish Civil War that the German Army gave orders to the Erma factory to design and produce a reliable and easily manufactured sub-machine gun, mainly for use by armoured and airborne troops. That same year the MP 38 appeared, the first arm of its type ever to be made entirely from metal and plastic. With its folding tubular metal stock and a receiver of steel tube, it was the first of a family which included the MP 40. This successor was of similar appearance but made more extensive use of pressing, spot-welding and brazing. A safety device was introduced too, it having been found that a jolt was often enough to bounce the bolt and fire a round. Oddly enough the famous Hugo Schmeisser had no hand in the MP 38's design; his factory made the MP 40 and the name stuck thereafter.

Germany
HECKLER & KOCH MP5

This excellent and highly reliable weapon is the chosen sub-machine gun of most of the world's elite military units. Their specialist requirements has meant the development of some 30 versions of the MP5. It is a delayed blowback weapon and the bolt is locked at the moment of firing. Super accurate, it is ideal for hostage rescue and in capable hands it can match a rifle at 100m. The basic mechanical design follows that of the G3 in which rearward movement of the bolt is delayed by rollers, and like the G3 it has a fluted chamber that lets propellant gas flow past the cartridge case. A curved magazine is now the standard and the gun fires in one of several modes: full auto, semi-auto, or three-round bursts. In addition it has an impressive list of accessories.

Below left: Loved by German soldiers the MP40 was often preferred by the Allies too.

Below: The MP5 is an ideal weapon for hostage rescue, as this SAS trooper demonstrates.

Great Britain
LANCHESTER MARK I

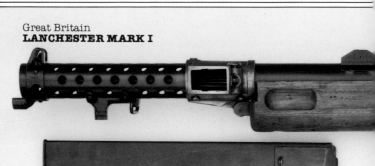

A hastily-produced copy of the German MP 28 to meet Britain's need in 1940; designed by George Lanchester. Most were issued to the Royal Navy, remaining in service for many years.

Great Britain
STEN MARK I

Note the cone-shaped flash hider and the somewhat crude forward pistol grip (folding forward beneath the barrel when not in use) of the first Mark of the famous utility weapon of 1941.

LANCHESTER MARK I

Length:	33·5" (851mm)
Weight:	9·65lb (4·38kg)
Barrel:	7·9" (200mm)
Calibre:	9mm
Rifling:	6 groove r/hand
Feed:	50-round box
C. Rate:	600 rpm
Muz Vel:	1200 f/s (365 m/s)
Sights:	Tangent. 600 yds

STEN MARK I

Length:	35·25" (896mm)
Weight:	7·21lb (3·27kg)
Barrel:	7·8" (198mm)
Calibre:	9mm
Rifling:	6 groove r/hand
Feed:	32-round box
C. Rate:	550 rpm
Muz Vel:	1200 f/s (365 m/s)
Sights:	Fixed

9mm Parabellum
9mm SAA Ball

·303" SAA Ball

Great Britain
LANCHESTER MARK I

In June 1940 Great Britain was in a very serious situation. Her expeditionary force had been compelled to make a hasty evacuation, mainly through Dunkirk, leaving behind it the bulk of its heavy weapons, and there was a very real risk that the victorious German Army would invade the country. One of the weapons which had belatedly impressed the British military authorities was the sub-machine gun, but although large numbers had been ordered from the United States there was no British model available. Arrangements were therefore hastily made to copy the German MP 28 which was known to be reliable, and a British version was designed by Mr George Lanchester of the Sterling Armament Company, after whom the completed weapon was named.

The new weapon was at first intended for the Royal Air Force and the Royal Navy, and in the event most of them went to the latter. The Lanchester, which bore an obvious resemblance to its parent arm, was a robust and reliable gun; British industry had not then been converted to a war footing so that the machining and finish of the weapon was of a very high quality, with a rifle type walnut stock (complete with brass buttplate), and a brass magazine housing. It was also fitted with a standard and boss to allow the ordinary Lee Enfield bayonet to be fixed if necessary.

It had a simple blowback mechanism and could fire either single rounds or automatic as required. It functioned well with most of the standard makes of 9mm rimless cartridge with the exception of the one for the Beretta. There was also a later Mark I which only fired automatic. The Lanchester saw little real service except with the occasional boat or landing party, but it remained in service with the Royal Navy for a long time. Many years after the war most HM ships carried racks of them, chained for security, though rarely used.

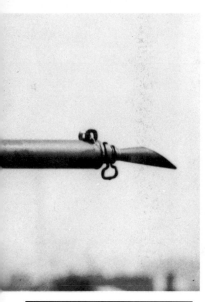

Above: *German PoW escorted by sailor with Lanchester Mark I.*

Above left: *British soldier fires Sten Mark 1 from shoulder.*

Great Britain
STEN MARK I

By mid-1941 large numbers of sub-machine guns were arriving from the United States. Great Britain and the Commonwealth were, however, engaged in raising and equipping new armies and in addition there were urgent demands for supplies and replacements for North and East Africa where British and Colonial troops were operating against the Italians. It was thus clear that there was an urgent requirement for a simple, home-produced sub-machine gun, and by the middle of 1941 a weapon had not only been designed but was in limited production and undergoing user trials. This was the famous Sten, which took its name from the initial letters of the surnames of the two people most closely concerned with its development Major (later Colonel) Shepherd who was a director of the Birmingham Small Arms Company and Mr Turpin, the principal designer, allied to the first two letters of

Enfield, the location of the Royal Small Arms factory where it was first produced. As soon as the few inevitable weaknesses revealed by the trials had been rectified the Sten gun went into large-scale production and in its various forms was to provide an invaluable source of additional automatic fire power to the British forces.

The Sten worked on a simple blow-back system using a heavy bolt with a coiled return spring, but in spite of its simple concept the first models made were still relatively elaborate, with a cone-shaped flash hider and a rather crude forward pistol grip which could be folded up underneath the barrel when not in use. It could fire either single shots or bursts, the change lever being a circular stud above the trigger. It also had some woodwork at the fore-end and as a bracer at the small of the butt.

113

Great Britain
STEN GUN MARK 2

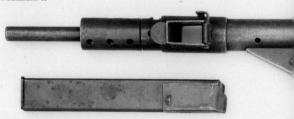

Utilitarian to the point of crudity, the Sten Mark 2 was probably
the ugliest weapon ever used by the British Army. Nevertheless,
it gave good service during World War II.

Great Britain
STEN GUN MARK 2 (SECOND PATTERN)

This Sten, made at the famous Long Branch factory in Canada, has
a somewhat better finish than the weapon above. Note its
bayonet: examples of this type are now very rare.

STEN GUN MARK 2	
Length:	30" (762mm)
Weight:	6·65lb (3kg)
Barrel:	7·75" (197mm)
Calibre:	9mm
Rifling:	6/2 groove r/hand
Feed:	32-round box
C. Rate:	550 rpm
Muz Vel:	1200 f/s (365 m/s)
Sights:	Fixed

STEN GUN MARK 2 (SECOND PATTERN)	
Length:	30" (762mm)
Weight:	6·65lb (3kg)
Barrel:	7·75" (197mm)
Calibre:	9mm
Rifling:	2 or 5 groove r/hand
Feed:	32-round box
C. Rate:	550 rpm
Muz Vel:	1200 f/s (365 m/s)
Sights:	Fixed

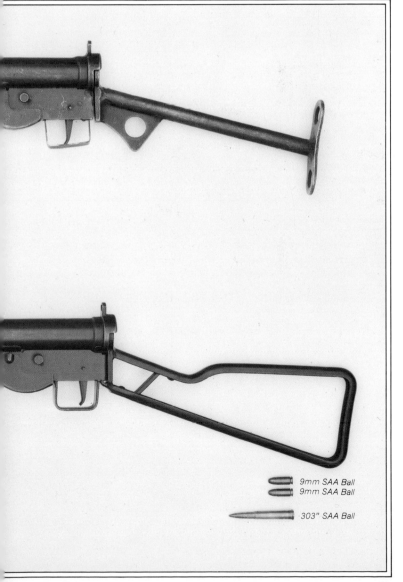

9mm SAA Ball
9mm SAA Ball

·303" SAA Ball

Great Britain
STEN GUN MARK 2

Towards the end of 1941 a modified version of the Sten Mark I appeared in the form of the Mark 2, this being the first of a long series of changes in the general design of the weapon. The Mark 2 was basically a somewhat stripped-down version of the Mark I, the intention being to simplify manufacturing processes wherever possible. The British gun trade had always prided itself on the finish of its weapons almost as much as on their effectiveness, and the tradition of machined and blued metal allied with polished walnut was a strong one. Nevertheless Great Britain was by this time fighting very literally for her existence and had therefore reached the inevitable conclusion that in emergencies, appearance was not important, only effectiveness, which set a fashion particularly in world sub-machine guns, for many years afterwards. This resulted in the Sten gun Mark 2, the ugliest, nastiest weapon ever used by the British Army. It looked cheap because it was cheap, with its great unfiled blobs of crude welding metal, its general appearance of scrap-iron, and its tendency to fall to pieces if dropped onto a hard surface. Nevertheless it worked, and not only worked but managed to incorporate one or two improvements, notably by attaching the magazine housing to a rotatable sleeve, held by a spring, so that in bad conditions it could be turned upwards through 90° thus acting as a dust cover for the ejection opening. This was a most useful refinement at a time when the British Army

was engaged in large-scale fighting in North Africa. Although the British Army, accustomed to its high quality Short Magazine Lee Enfield rifles and handsomely finished Bren light machine guns, joked about their 'tin Tommy-gun' they got good value out of it. Perhaps one of the most persistent weaknesses in the make-up of the wartime Sten gun was in the relatively poor quality of its magazine, although in the circumstances of hasty construction with poor metal this is not altogether to be wondered at. In particular the lips were very susceptible to damage, which had a serious effect on the feed and led to endless stoppages. It was also found that the dirt and dust inseparable from the fighting in the Western desert, tended to clog the magazine, and although careful attention to cleanliness helped in this respect the problem was never really solved with this particular weapon. Despite these drawbacks, the Mark 2 was an important weapon.

Great Britain
**STEN GUN MARK 2
(SECOND PATTERN)**

The British and Colonial forces appeared to have an insatiable appetite for Sten guns. Over one hundred thousand of the earlier Marks had been produced by early 1942 and there was still no slackening of the demand. Apart from the inevitable loss and damage in action, more and more troops were being raised and trained, and as the prospect of an invasion of North West Europe, with the probability of extensive street fighting in towns and villages, drew closer the need for sub-machine guns continued to increase.

Apart from the regular armies there was also an increasing demand for light, easily concealed automatic weapons from the various Resistance movements in occupied Europe so that production had to be increased accordingly. There was, however, an equal need for other weapons too, so that no priority could be given. All that could be done was to pare and reduce and simplify so that three weapons could be produced with the same effort and little more than the same *matériel,* that had produced two previously. Much help was given by some of the Dominions, notably Canada, and the weapon illustrated is an example of the type made there at the famous Long Branch factory. Although made to similar specifications to the British version, it is of somewhat better finish, with a more robust skeleton butt. It also has a bayonet, details of which are clearly shown in the illustration, and examples of this are now very rare.

Perhaps appropriately this type was first used in action on the ill-fated Dieppe raid of 19 August, 1942 in which the Canadian Army fought gallantly.

Below left: *Free French soldier in training with Sten Mark 2.*

Below: *British Home Guard men receive instruction from soldier with Sten Mark 2 (Second Pattern), with bayonet fixed.*

Great Britain
STEN GUN MARK 6(S)

The Mark 2 silencer fitted to this arm, which was largely used by special forces, tended to heat rapidly; hence the canvas hand guard fitted over its rear area.

Australia
OWEN MACHINE CARBINE

Designed for use in the jungles of the Far East during World War II, the magazine of the Owen is set vertically above the gun, facilitating the user's movement through thick cover.

STEN GUN MARK 6(S)

Length (s):	35·75″ (908mm)
Weight:	9·8lb (4·45kg)
Barrel:	7·80″ (198mm)
Calibre:	9mm
Rifling:	6 groove r/hand
Feed:	32-round box
C. Rate:	550 rpm
Muz Vel:	c1000 f/s (305 m/s)
Sights:	Fixed

OWEN MACHINE CARBINE

Length:	32″ (813mm)
Weight:	9·35lb (4·24kg)
Barrel:	9·75″ (250mm)
Calibre:	9mm
Rifling:	7 groove r/hand
Feed:	32-round box
C. Rate:	700 rpm
Muz Vel:	1375 f/s (420 m/s)
Sights:	Fixed. offset

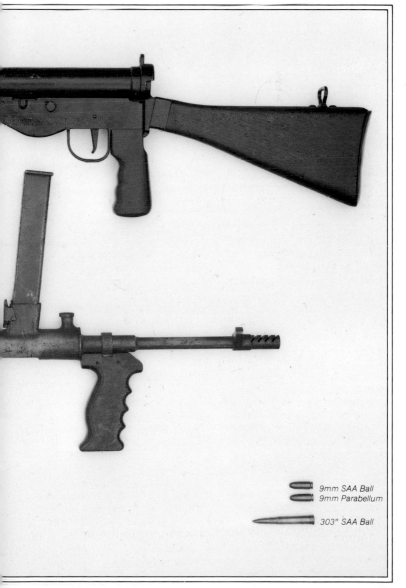

9mm SAA Ball
9mm Parabellum

303″ SAA Ball

A British Army sergeant fires a Sten Gun Mark 6(S) fitted with an extremely complex sniper scope. This silenced arm was in use as late as 1953.

Great Britain
STEN GUN MARK 6(S)

The Mark 2 Sten, which has already been described, probably marked the lowest point in the gun's history, and thereafter quality began to improve. Practically all components were still made in small factories and workshops with no previous connection with the manufacture of firearms, but, perhaps due to experience, the general finish was markedly better than in the early days. There was a Mark 3 (similar in appearance to the Mark 2) which was made in huge numbers and this was followed by a Mark 4, which never went into full scale production. This in turn was followed by probably the best Sten of all, the Mark 5, which was to see service from 1944 until well into the 1950s. Although very similar to its predecessors it was of more robust construction with a wooden butt (some with brass buttplates) and pistol grip. and provision was made for it to take the standard bayonet. Experiments had been conducted earlier with a silenced Mark 6 Sten which was sufficiently successful to attract the admiration of Colonel Skorzeny, the famous German who rescued Mussolini, and in 1944 it was decided that a weapon of this type was again required. The standard Mark 2 silencer was thus fitted to the Mark 5, which was then re-designated Mark 6(S). The muzzle velocity of the Mark 5 bullet was in excess of the speed of sound which posed a number of problems in connection with the 'sonic boom' effect, but by drilling gas escape holes in the barrel the velocity was brought down to the required figure. The silencer tended to heat rapidly so a canvas hand guard was laced over it. It was not considered advisable to fire bursts through the silencer except in extreme emergencies. The Mark 6 Sten was used mainly by airborne forces and Resistance fighters in World War II and as late as 1953.

Australia
OWEN MACHINE CARBINE

When Japan entered World War II on the side of the Axis powers, Australia found herself in a precarious position. Most of her small army was engaged in the Middle East and her vast and sparsely inhabited country presented a most attractive target to a warlike race seeking living room. Although there was a well established arms factory in existence at Lithgow, Australia was not then a very industrialized country, but she began to produce arms as a matter of hard necessity. One of her first efforts was an Australian Sten, known, perhaps inevitably, as the Austen, but although by no means a bad weapon it was never popular with the Australian Army. The first locally designed sub machine gun was the work of Lieutenant E. Owen, of the Australian Army, which was adopted in November, 1941 and put into production immediately. It was a well made weapon, if a little on the heavy side, and was an immediate success with the soldiers. It was of fairly orthodox design and its point of balance was immediately above the pistol grip which allowed it to be fired one-handed if necessary. The magazine was vertically above the gun and although this involved offset sights the idea was popular because it helped when moving through thick cover. All Owens were camouflaged after 1943 and provision was made for a bayonet in 1944. The Owen was a thoroughly good weapon and was still in use in the 1960s.

A civilian technician fires the Australian Owen Machine Carbine. Note that, unlike the weapon shown on the colour spread, the metal bodywork between butt and trigger-grip has not been cut away.

Great Britain
BSA EXPERIMENTAL 1949

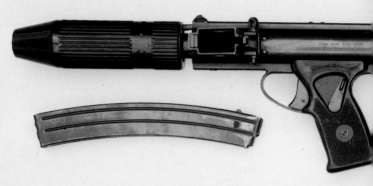

Designed to fit the British General Staff's specifications for an SMG to replace the Sten after World War II, BSA's unsuccessful candidate was cocked by the action of a rod actuated by twisting the plastic-covered fore-end grip.

Great Britain
MCEM 2

Another of the candidates to replace the Sten, this experimental weapon was designed in Britain by a Polish officer. Its butt, of canvas on a wire frame, serves as a holster when detached.

BSA EXPERIMENTAL 1949

Length:	27·9" (697mm)
Weight:	6·45lb (2·9kg)
Barrel:	8" (203mm)
Calibre:	9mm
Rifling:	6 groove r/hand
Feed:	32-round box
C. Rate:	600 rpm
Muz Vel:	1200 f/s (365 m/s)
Sights:	100/200 yds

MCEM 2

Length:	23·5" (598mm)
Weight	6lb (2·72kg)
Barrel:	8·5" (216mm)
Calibre:	9mm
Rifling:	6 groove r/hand
Feed:	18-round box
C. Rate:	1000 rpm .
Muz Vel:	1200 f/s (365 m/s)
Sights:	Fixed

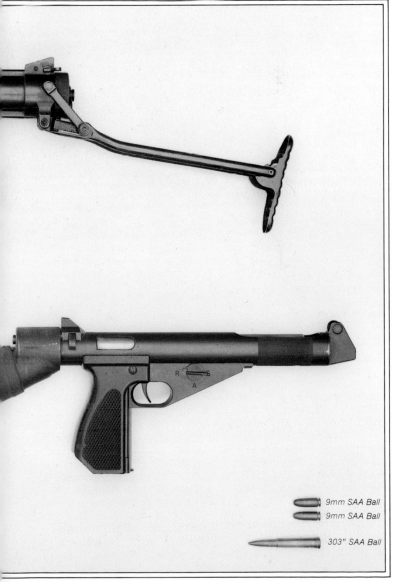

9mm SAA Ball

9mm SAA Ball

·303" SAA Ball

Great Britain
BSA EXPERIMENTAL 1949

The main British sub-machine gun during World War II was the famous Sten, which although hastily designed and roughly finished did its job very well. It was, however, a strictly wartime expedient and even before the war was quite over a new General Staff specification had been issued for a post-war sub-machine gun. This laid down the basic requirements that it should weigh a maximum of six pounds (2.72kg) without magazine, fire at not more than six hundred rounds per minute, have a magazine capacity of between thirty and sixty rounds, and take the No 5 rifle bayonet. Various tests were arranged between 1947 and 1952 for which a number of weapons were entered, among them the Birmingham Small Arms Company's weapon of the type illustrated. It was of conventional blowback mechanism, but was unusual in that it had no cocking handle, that function being performed by a flat rod attached to the plastic covered fore-end grip. When the grip was twisted and pushed forward the rod went with it and the end of it engaged the bolt which was then in the forward position. As the grip was pulled back the rod forced the bolt back also until it was caught by the sear, at which stage it disengaged from the rod. The gun also had another unusual feature in that the magazine housing could be released and swung forward on a hinge without removing the magazine, which was thought to facilitate the clearing of stoppages. It was fitted with a sturdy folding stock which did not interfere with the firing of

Above: *The 9mm Experimental sub-machine gun designed by the Birmingham Small Arms Company and tested, but not accepted, by the British Army in 1949-52, is fired from the shoulder.*

Above right: *The BSA Experimental 1949 SMG is fired from the hip. Curved magazine denotes late model.*

the gun when forward, and its change lever was situated above the left-hand pistol grip. Over the years there were a number of variations in the original design; the first model took a straight magazine, later ones being curved as illustrated, and as a result of a change in specification it was modified to take a bayonet. There were also variations in the shape of the forehand grip. The gun was not finally accepted for service and specimens of it are now quite rare.

Great Britain
MCEM 2

Although the Sten gun had served Great Britain well in the period 1941-45 it was not really of the quality required for the post-war army, and after the war was over tests began to find a suitable successor for it. A good deal of design work had been going on, both by native British designers and by a variety of Polish experts, so there was not likely to be any shortage of contenders. The series developed by Enfield were given the collective description of Military Carbine Experimental Models (MCEM), the various types being denoted by a serial number; as a matter of interest the first in the series was the work of Mr H. J. Turpin who had been instrumental in designing the original Sten gun. The weapon illustrated, the

MCEM 2, was the work of one of the rival designers, a Polish officer named Lieutenant Podsenkowsky, and it was in many ways an unusual weapon. It was under fifteen inches long and its magazine fitted into the pistol grip; it was also well balanced which meant that it could be fired one-handed like an automatic pistol. The bolt was of advanced design and consisted of a half cylinder 8½ inches (216mm) long with the striker at the rear, so that at the instant of firing almost the whole of the barrel was in fact inside it. There was a slot above the muzzle into which the firer placed his finger to draw the bolt back to cock it, and the gun had a wire-framed canvas holster which could also be used as a butt. It fired at a cyclic rate of one thousand rounds per minute which made it very hard to control and which may have led to its rejection.

Great Britain
STERLING L2A3

Australia
F1 SUB-MACHINE GUN

The butt of the F1 is a prolongation of the barrel. This makes
for accurate shooting, but also necessitates an elevated sight
line; hence the distinctive metal flap of the backsight.

STERLING L2A3

Length:	28" (800mm)
Weight:	6lb (2·75kg)
Barrel	7·8" (198mm)
Calibre:	9mm
Rifling:	6 groove r/hand
Feed:	32-round box
C. Rate:	550 rpm
Muz Vel:	1200 f/s (365 m/s)
Sights:	100 and 200 yds

F1 SUB-MACHINE GUN

Length:	28·1" (925mm)
Weight:	7·2lb (3·266kg)
Barrel:	8" (203mm)
Calibre:	9mm
Rifling:	6 groove r/hand
Feed:	34-round box
C. Rate:	600 rpm
Muz Vel:	1200 f/s (365 m/s)
Sights:	Fixed

Developed from 1942 onward this arm, then known as the Patchett after its designer, was extensively tested by the British Army from 1947 and was adopted to replace the Sten in 1953.

9mm SAA Ball
9mm Parabellum

·303" SAA Ball

Covered by a comrade with a Sterling L2A3 sub-machine gun, a British paratrooper enters a deserted house, in training.

Great Britain
STERLING L2A3

This gun was designed by a Mr George Patchett and was at first known as the Patchett sub-machine gun. It was originally patented in 1942 and by the end of the war a small number had been made by the Sterling Engineering Company, which had earlier been involved in the production of the Lanchester. A few of these early guns were used by British airborne troops towards the end of the war and their reports on them were encouraging. In the course of the search for a replacement for the Sten this gun was tested against various others in 1947; none was accepted as a result of this first trial because all were considered to need modification. By the time of the next trial in 1951 the Patchett, as it was still then called, was clearly the best gun of those available, and in September 1953 it was finally accepted for

service in the British Army. Its official title was the SMG L2A1, but from the date of its introduction it was commonly known as the Sterling. The gun, which is well made and finished, is of normal blowback mechanism but is unusual in having a ribbed bolt which cuts away dirt and fouling as it accumulates and forces it out of the receiver. This allows the gun to function well under the most adverse conditions. The gun underwent a good many modifications after its initial introduction, notably in the addition of foresight protections, varying shapes of muzzle and butt, and on one light version a spring-loaded bayonet. Some of the earlier models also took a straight magazine. The current version is the L2A3, and the standard Canadian SMG is closely based on it.

Australia
F1 SUB-MACHINE GUN

The standard sub-machine gun of the Australian Forces during World War II was the reliable and well tried Owen gun, which remained in service until 1962. In spite of its excellent reputation the Owen had certain drawbacks, principally its weight, its somewhat high cyclic rate of fire, and the fact that due to the exigencies of wartime manufacture many of its components were not interchangeable which made maintenance difficult. Before the war was over the Australians canvassed the views of many soldiers with battle experience as to what an ideal sub-machine gun should be, so that they had ample information on which to base any specifications for a new weapon. The first gun to be based on these ideas was similar in many ways to the Owen, but much lighter and with its magazine in the pistol grip. This model was not a success and was not developed. However, in 1959 and 1960 two further models were produced; these were known provisionally as the X1 and X2, and after minor modifications became the weapon illustrated, the F1. It was based largely on the original specification and is light in weight and with a much lower cyclic rate than its predecessor. It retains the top magazine of the Owen which was universally popular, although it requires offset sights. The backsight is a shaped metal flap which folds forward over the receiver when not required. The height of this sight is made necessary because the butt is a prolongation of the barrel, which makes for accurate shooting but which requires the sight line to be high. The cocking handle, which is on the left of the body, has a cover attached to it to keep dirt out of the cocking slot. Although the cocking handle is normally non-reciprocating, the F1 incorporates a device by which it can be made to engage the bolt. This means that if the mechanism becomes jammed with dirt the bolt can be worked backwards and forwards by means of the handle in order to loosen it. The pistol grip is a standard rifle component.

The Australian F1 sub-machine gun: note height of the shaped metal flap of the backsight.

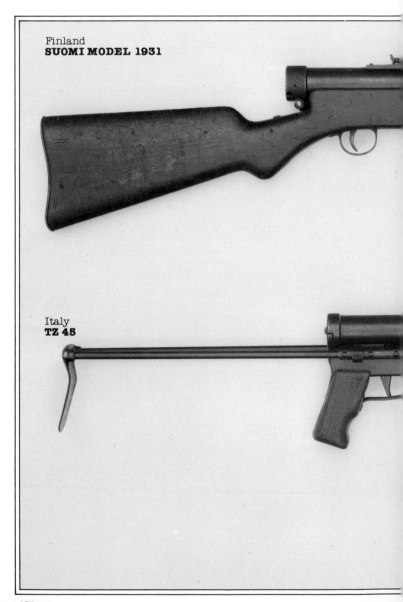

Finland
SUOMI MODEL 1931

Italy
TZ 45

Length:	34·25" (870mm)
Weight:	10·34lb (4·69kg)
Barrel:	12·5" (317mm)
Calibre:	9mm
Rifling:	6 groove r/hand
Feed:	(See text)
C. Rate:	900 rpm
Muz Vel:	1312 f/s (400 m/s)
Sights:	110-547 yds

Length:	33·5" (851mm)
Weight:	7·20lb (3·26kg)
Barrel:	9" (229mm)
Calibre:	9mm
Rifling:	6 groove r/hand
Feed:	20/40-round box
C. Rate:	550 rpm
Muz Vel:	1250 f/s (365 m/s)
Sights:	Fixed

Designed by Johannes Lahti, the Suomi entered service with the
Finnish Army in 1931. It was a reliable, robust arm, but very
heavy by modern standards.

The rough and ready appearance of the TZ 45, designed by the
Giandoso brothers, is explained by its genesis in war-time Italy. It
appeared in 1945 and only about 6,000 were made.

9mm Parabellum
9mm Parabellum

·303" SAA Ball

Finland
SUOMI MODEL 1931

Suomi is the native word for Finland, and the first of the series bearing the name was developed from 1922 onwards which makes it one of the earliest sub-machine guns to appear. It was designed by the well-known Finnish designer Johannes Lahti, and the first finished models appeared in 1926. They were effective but very complex weapons, designed to fire the 7·62mm Parabellum cartridge from a magazine with such a pronounced curve that three of them placed end to end formed a complete circle. This gun was only produced in very small numbers and is thus chiefly of interest because it was the first of a series. The model illustrated was also designed by Lahti, but although it retained some of the features of the Model 26, so many changes were made that it was virtually a new weapon. Although patents were not finally granted until 1932 the gun was in use by the Finnish Army in the previous year, hence its final designation of Model 31. It worked by normal blowback system and had no less than four different magazines, a single 20-round box, a double 50-round box, and two drums, one of 40-round capacity and one of 71. Like most sub-machine guns of its vintage it was very well made of good steel, heavily machined and milled and unusually well finished. The end product was therefore an exceptionally reliable and robust weapon and although it was very heavy by modern standards (with the bigger drum magazine it weighed over fifteen pounds) this at least had the merit of reducing recoil and vibration and thus increasing its accuracy, for which it was very well known.

It was made under licence in Sweden, Denmark, and Switzerland, and apart from Finland was also used by Sweden, Switzerland and Norway and to a lesser extent Poland. It is still used in many units of the Finnish Army, although all surviving weapons have been modified to take a modern 36-round box magazine of improved pattern. At the end of 1939 the Russians, having failed to persuade the Finns to make some territorial adjustments to enhance Soviet security, invaded Finland. The Finns fought bravely and made good use of the Suomi.

A Finnish soldier fires his Suomi Model 1931 SMG; in this case fed from a drum magazine.

Italy
TZ 45

So many Italian sub-machine guns have been produced by the famous Brescian firm of Beretta that it sometimes comes as something of a surprise to people to find an Italian weapon of this type produced by some other firm. World War II, however, saw the appearance of a considerable variety of other weapons, the TZ 45 being amongst them. It was designed by the Giandoso brothers as a wartime expedient and first went into limited production in 1945. This new gun, which worked on the normal blowback system, was very crudely made and finished, partly of roughly machined parts and partly of stampings. This is not surprising in view of its date of manufacture, by which time the quality of most other countries' products had dropped

correspondingly. One of the interesting features of this gun is that it incorporates a grip safety; this consists of an L-shaped lever just behind the magazine housing (which also acts as a forward hand grip). Firm pressure on the vertical part of the lever (which is clearly visible in the photograph) causes the horizontal arm to be depressed sufficiently to withdraw an upper stud from the bolt way, thus allowing the working parts to function. This device which was similar to the one employed on some models of the Danish Madsen sub-machine gun, was a useful one, but it did of course prevent the weapon being used single-handed. The TZ 45 had a retractable stock, made of light tubing; when pushed in the front ends engaged in holes in a plate below the barrel about six inches (153mm) from the muzzle. Although probably not specifically intended for the

purpose it presumably also acted as a stop to prevent the weapon being pulled back from a port in an armoured vehicle by some sudden jolt, rather like the attachment on the German 'Schmeisser'. There are two parallel slots cut into the top of the barrel at the muzzle end which act as a crude but moderately effective compensator. Although it was an adequate weapon the TZ 45 came too late in the war to be of much use and only about six thousand were made. These were chiefly used by Italian troops on internal security duties including the rounding up of the armed deserters of half-a-dozen nationalities who had happily taken to banditry in the last months of the war. After the war the gun was offered commercially on the world market, but only the Burmese showed interest, a number being locally made there in the early 1950s. These guns were manu-factured under the title BA 52.

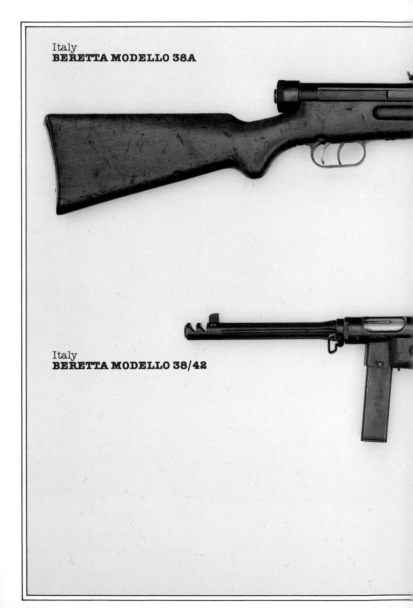

Italy
BERETTA MODELLO 38A

Italy
BERETTA MODELLO 38/42

BERETTA MODELLO 38A

Length:	37·25" (946mm)
Weight:	9·25lb (4·97kg)
Barrel:	12·4" (315mm)
Calibre:	9mm
Rifling:	6 groove r/hand
Feed:	10/20/40-round box
C. Rate:	600 rpm
Muz Vel:	1378 f/s (420 m/s)
Sights:	547 yds (500m)

BERETTA MODELLO 38/42

Length:	31·5" (800mm)
Weight:	7·20lb (3·26kg)
Barrel:	8·4" (216mm)
Calibre:	9mm
Rifling:	6 groove r/hand
Feed:	20/40-round box
C. Rate:	550 rpm
Muz Vel:	1250 f/s (381 m/s)
Sights:	219 yds (200m)

This was probably the most successful of the sub-machine guns designed for Beretta by Tullio Marengoni; it was extensively used by the Italian and German armies during World War II.

The Marengoni-designed Modello 38/42 is largely a utility version of the Modello 38 — simplified to conform to mass-production methods. Like the earlier weapon, it had a forward trigger for single rounds and a rear one for firing bursts.

9mm Parabellum
9mm Parabellum
·303" SAA Ball

135

Italy
BERETTA MODELLO 38A

The Northern Italian firm of
Beretta had a deservedly high
reputation for its sub-machine
guns, most of which have been
designed by their most talented
engineer, Tullio Marengoni,
who worked for them for many
years. Among the weapons he
produced was the Modello 38A
which probably has good claims
to be regarded as his most
successful sub-machine gun. It
had its origins in a self-loading
carbine which was first
produced in small numbers for
police use in 1935, but which
by 1938 had been improved to
the point where it could be
manufactured as a true sub-
machine gun. It came of
course far too early for the
mass-production techniques
developed a few years later and
was made to the high pre-war
standards customary among
gun makers. It was therefore
well machined and finished
which made it expensive to
produce, but which resulted in
a most reliable and accurate
arm. It functioned by normal
blowback and had a separate
firing pin, again a somewhat

unusual refinement. Its forward
trigger was for single shots, the
other for bursts. The first model
can be distinguised by the
elongated slots in its jacket,
by its compensator, which
consisted of a single large hole
in the top of the muzzle with a
bar across it, and by the fact
that it was fitted with a folding,
knife-type bayonet. Not many of
these were produced before
the elongated cooling slots
were replaced by round holes,
which thereafter remained
standard. The third version,
which is the one illustrated, was
mainly distinguished by the
absence of a bayonet and by its
new compensator consisting of
four separate cuts across the
muzzle. This version remained
as the production model for the
remainder of the war, although
there are some minor con-
cessions to the principles of
mass-production, notably in the
use of a pressed and welded
jacket. This version was used
extensively by both the Italian
and the German armies, and
captured specimens were
popular with Allied soldiers.
The Beretta Modello 38A was
also used by a number of
countries, notably Romania
and Argentina.

Italian soldiers during World War II, with slung Beretta Modello 38A sub-machine guns. The man on the left has in place on his weapon what appears to be the 20-round box magazine.

Italy
BERETTA MODELLO 38/42

After a year or so of war the Italians, like all other combatants, soon realized that they would have to accept modern mass-production methods if their supplies of war *matériel* were to keep pace with demand. As far as sub-machine guns were concerned, this realization resulted in the Beretta Modello 38/42, which like most of its predecessors was invented by Marengoni, and which came into full production in 1942. It was for all practical purposes a utility version of the earlier Modello 38, although it also incorporated a number of features from another sub-machine gun, the Modello 1, which had been designed, needless to say by Marengoni, in 1941 as a weapon for airborne forces on the lines of the German MP 40, but which had never gone into production due to its complicated construction. The whole weapon had also of course been considerably simplified to conform to modern mass-production methods, but in spite of this it was an efficient and popular gun. As far as external appearances were concerned there were a number of differences. The rifle-type stock, athough similar, was cut short at the magazine housing, and the adjustable rearsight disappeared, as did the perforated jacket which had been such a notable feature of many Beretta guns. The barrel had deep parallel fluting along its whole length, this being

intended to assist the dissipation of heat in the absence of the jacket, while the compensator was reduced to two cuts only instead of the previous four. The bolt was somewhat simplified with a fixed firing pin integral with it instead of the separate mechanism previously used. The main return spring worked on a rod, the end of which extended appreciably beyond the rear of the receiver, and as before the gun had two triggers, the forward one for single rounds, the rear one for bursts. The cocking handle, which does not move with the bolt, had a dust cover attached to it to keep the internal mechanism as clear as possible. The general appearance of the gun was utilitarian as compared with its predecessors, stampings and welding having been used wherever possible, although the finish was surprisingly good and the whole weapon strong and serviceable. Later productions had plain barrels instead of the distinctive fluted ones and were sometimes referred to as the Modello 38/44. There was a later variation still, in which the weight and dimensions of the bolt were reduced; this led in turn to a somewhat shorter return spring and rod, which did not protrude beyond the rear of the receiver as in the earlier models. The date that this model went into production is not very clear, but most of them seem to have come off the assembly lines after the end of the war so that its designation 38/44 is somewhat in doubt. The Beretta 38/42 was widely used by the Italians and Germans and after the war a number of the 38/44 Model were sold to various countries including Syria and Pakistan.

People's Republic of China
TYPE 50

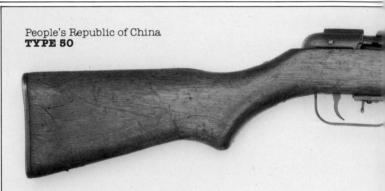

The Chinese received many Soviet PPSh 41 SMGs in 1949 and had begun manufacture of this copy – nicknamed the "burp gun", from its rate of fire, in the Korean War – by 1950.

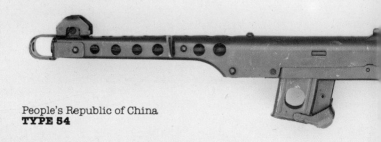

People's Republic of China
TYPE 54

Chinese copies of the Soviet PPS 43 are distinguishable from the original arms only by the designs (in this case, a diamond) incised in the plastic pistol grips.

TYPE 50	
Length:	33·75" (858mm)
Weight:	8lb (3·63kg)
Barrel:	10·75" (273mm)
Calibre:	7·62mm
Rifling:	4 groove r/hand
Feed:	35-round box
C. Rate:	900 rpm
Muz Vel:	1400 f/s (472 m/s)
Sights:	110-219 yds

TYPE 54	
Length:	32·25" (819mm)
Weight:	7·4lb (3·36kg)
Barrel:	10" (254mm)
Calibre:	7·62mm
Rifling:	4 groove r/hand
Feed:	35-round box
C. Rate:	700 rpm
Muz Vel:	1600 f/s (488 m/s)
Sights:	Flip. 110-219 yds

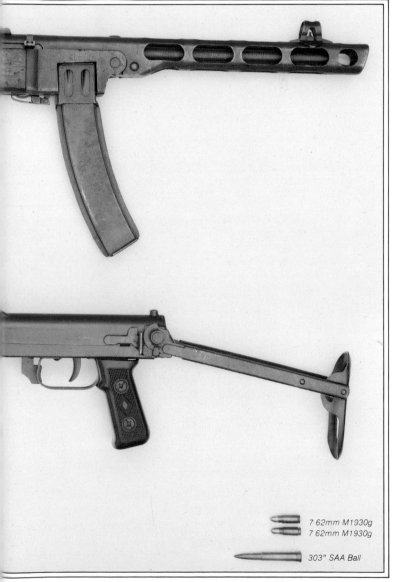

7·62mm M1930g
7·62mm M1930g
·303" SAA Ball

People's Republic of China
TYPE 50

Like many of the weapons used by Communist China, their sub-machine gun Type 50 had its origins in a weapon first produced by the Soviet Union, in this case the PPSh 41. As with most other combatant nations the Russians soon saw the need for mass production and the new gun was largely made of heavy gauge stampings, welded, pinned and brazed as necessary. The gun was of normal blowback mechanism and had the interior of the barrel chromed, a fairly common Soviet device. One of its distinctive features is that the front end of the perforated barrel casing slopes steeply backward from top to bottom, thus acting as a compensator to keep the muzzle down. In spite of its high cyclic rate of fire the gun was reasonably accurate and could be fired in single rounds if required. The earliest versions had a tangent backsight but this was soon replaced by a simpler flip sight. The Chinese Communists received many of these guns in and after 1949 and started their own large scale manufacture of them in 1949 or 1950. Their version was essentially similar to its Russian counterpart, but had a somewhat lighter stock. It is also designed to take a curved box magazine though it will also fire the 71-round drum which was the standard magazine on the original Russian model. All Chinese versions have the two-range flip sight. The first locally-made weapons were crude in the extreme and gave the impression of having been made by apprentice blacksmiths (as perhaps they

were). Nevertheless they worked, which was the first and only requirement of the Chinese. The Type 50 was used extensively by the Chinese in the Korean war where it earned the inelegant but expressive nickname 'burp-gun' from its high rate of fire. Many were also used against the French in Indo-China in the 1950s.

People's Republic of China
TYPE 54

The origins of this particular weapon are unusual, since it was designed by A. Sudarev at Leningrad in 1942 when the city was under actual blockade by the Germans. Arms were in short supply and as none could be brought in it became necessary to improvise from local resources. The new gun, originally known as the Russian PPS 42, was therefore made in the city itself, so that weapons coming off the production line

were liable to be used in action in a matter of hours. As was to be expected the gun was made of stampings, using any suitable grade of metal, and was held together by riveting, welding, and pinning. Nevertheless it was not only cheap but it turned out to be effective. It worked on the usual simple blowback system and would only fire automatic; perhaps its oddest feature was its semi-circular compensator, which helped to keep the muzzle down but increased blast considerably. This was followed by the PPS 43, modified and improved by the same engineer who had been responsible for the earlier model. Its most unusual feature was that it had no separate ejector in the normal sense of the word. The bolt moved backwards and forwards along a guide rod which was of such a length that as the bolt came back with the empty case, the end of the rod

caught it a sharp blow and knocked it clear.

After the Chinese revolution of 1949, the Soviet Union naturally supplied its new ally with a considerable quantity of arms including large numbers of the PPS 43, and by 1953 the Chinese had begun large-scale manufacture of these weapons, virtually unchanged in appearance from the Russian prototypes. The only way in which it can be distinguished is by the fact that the plastic pistol grips often bear a large letter K in a central design. This, however, is by no means universal and other designs, including a diamond, may be found. The gun is still often found in South East Asia.

A soldier of the People's Republic of China receives instruction in the 7.62mm Type 54 sub-machine gun, a direct copy of the Soviet PPS 43. The Chinese lay great emphasis on aquatic training; hence this unusual firing position.

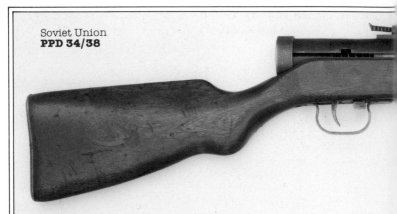

Soviet Union
PPD 34/38

The PPD (**P**istolet-**P**ulemyot, or sub-machine gun, designed by
Vasily **D**egtyaryev) was fed from a drum magazine (right)
holding 71 rounds and operated by a clockwork mechanism.

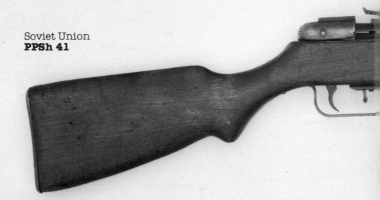

Soviet Union
PPSh 41

The PPSh (**P**istolet-**P**ulemyot designed by Georgi **Sh**pagin) was mass-
produced from 1942 onward. Whole battalions of the Soviet armies
carried sub-machine guns and total production exceeded 5 million.

PPD 34/38		PPSh 41	
Length	30·6" (779mm)	**Length:**	33·1" (841mm)
Weight:	8·25lb (3·74kg)	**Weight:**	8·0lb (3·63kg)
Barrel:	10·75" (272mm)	**Barrel**	10·6" (269mm)
Calibre:	7·62mm	**Calibre:**	7·62mm
Rifling:	4 groove r/hand	**Rifling:**	4 groove r/hand
Feed:	71-round drum	**Feed:**	71 drum/35 box
C. Rate:	800 rpm	**C. Rate:**	900 rpm
Muz Vel:	1600 f/s (489 m/s)	**Muz Vel:**	1600 f/s (489 m/s)
Sights:	547 yds (500m)	**Sights:**	547 yds (500m)

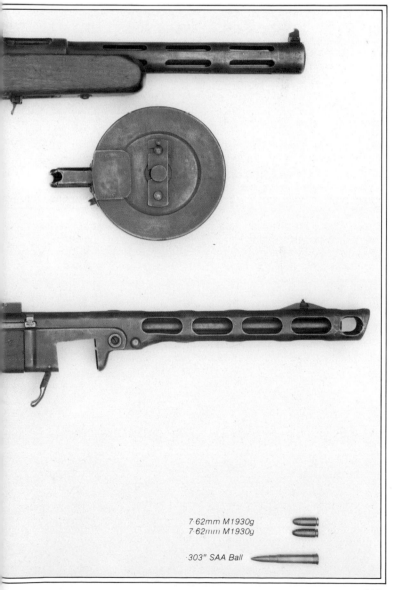

7·62mm M1930g
7·62mm M1930g

·303" SAA Ball

Soviet Union
PPD 34/38

This weapon was designed by Vasily Degtyaryev, the well-known Soviet expert on automatic weapons, and the D in the title is his initial, the PP standing for Pistolet-Pulemyot, the usual Russian term for what we know as a sub-machine gun. It initially appeared in 1934 and may be regarded as the first really successful weapon of its type to be used in the Soviet Army.

It was based fairly closely on the German MP28.II, and coming before the days of mass-production was reasonably well made and finished by the standards of Russian industry as it then was. The PPD worked by normal blowback on the open bolt principle single rounds or bursts being obtained by the use of a selector in front of the trigger. Both bore and chamber were chromed to prevent undue wear. The cartridges were fed from a near-vertical drum with an unusual extension piece which fitted into the bottom of the receiver; this drum, which was worked by clockwork, was very similar mechanically to that of the Finnish Suomi, and held seventy-one rounds. This gave the soldier using it a good reserve of fire without having to reload, but made the gun heavy. As drum magazines are susceptible to dirt, there were probably also problems over stoppages; there was in fact also a curved box magazine but this was very rarely used. One or two minor variations to the original model were made, the most obvious being the reduction in the number of jacket slots from rows of eight small ones to three larger ones. Although the gun was technically replaced by the PPD 40 in 1940 it was used in the Finnish campaigns and probably also saw later service elsewhere.

Red Army soldiers with a knocked-out German AFV during World War II. Those at centre and right have PPD 34/38 sub-machine guns.

Tank-mounted Russian scouts with PPSh 41 sub-machine guns; note that these have drum magazines.

Soviet Union
PPSh 41

At the outbreak of World War II in 1939, the Soviet Army was armed with the PPD 34/38, but by the beginning of 1940 this was gradually being replaced by a modified version of the PPD 40 which was similar in appearance but took a different type of drum. Almost immediately the gun illustrated was put into limited production, and after stringent testing by the Russian Army was finally approved early in 1942, after which production was on a vast scale. It was designed by Georgii Shpagin, another well-known Russian expert, and this fact is denoted by the inclusion of his initial in the official designation of the new gun. The PPSh was an early and successful example of the application of mass-production techniques to the manufacture of firearms, a change made essential by the Soviet Union's huge military commitments at that time. As far as possible it was made from sheet metal stampings, welding and riveting being used wherever feasible, and although it retained the rather old-fashioned looking wooden butt it was a sturdy and reliable arm. It worked on the usual blowback system with a buffer at the rear end of the receiver to reduce vibration and had a selector lever in front of the trigger to give single rounds or burst as required. As its cyclic rate of fire was high and would have tended to make the muzzle rise when firing bursts, the front of the barrel jacket was sloped backwards so as to act as a compensator, a simple and reasonably successful expedient. Feed for the PPSh was either by a seventy-one round drum, basically similar to that of the earlier PPD series but not interchangeable with them, or by a thirty-five round box. In order to reduce wear and help cleaning, the bore and chamber of these guns were all chromed. There appear to have been only two basic models of this gun; the first model, the one illustrated, had a somewhat complicated tangent backsight, while the second one made do with a perfectly adequate two aperture flip sight. The Soviet armies greatly favoured the sub-machine gun and on occasions whole battalions were armed with it, so it is not surprising that the total numbers manufactured should have exceeded five million. It was also widely copied by other Communist countries, and although long obsolete in the Soviet Union itself it is probably still extensively used elsewhere. The Chinese in particular copied it as their Type 50 and must themselves have produced it in vast numbers.

Sweden
CARL GUSTAV MODEL 45

Switzerland
REXIM-FAVOR

One of the many variations of the SMG (at one time known as the Favor and probably made under contract in Spain) produced by the Rexim Small Arms Company, Geneva, from 1953 onward.

CARL GUSTAV MODEL 45		REXIM-FAVOR	
Length:	31·8" (808mm)	**Length:**	32·0" (813mm)
Weight	7·62lb (3·45kg)	**Weight**	7·0lb (3·18kg)
Barrel:	8·0" (203mm)	**Barrel:**	10·75" (273mm)
Calibre:	9mm	**Calibre:**	9mm
Rifling:	6 groove r/hand	**Rifling:**	5 groove r/hand
Feed:	36/50-round box	**Feed:**	20-round box
C. Rate:	600 rpm	**C. Rate:**	600 rpm
Muz Vel:	1210 f/s (369 m/s)	**Muz Vel:**	1300 f/s (396 m/s)
Sights:	328 yds (300m)	**Sights:**	Flip. 100/200 yds

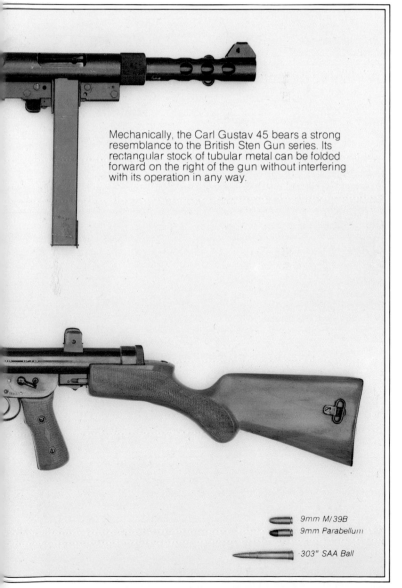

Mechanically, the Carl Gustav 45 bears a strong resemblance to the British Sten Gun series. Its rectangular stock of tubular metal can be folded forward on the right of the gun without interfering with its operation in any way.

9mm M/39B

9mm Parabellum

·303" SAA Ball

Sweden
CARL GUSTAV MODEL 45

Sweden did not adopt a sub-
machine gun until 1937, when
she began to manufacture a
slightly modified form of the
Finnish Suomi, which was
made under licence by the Carl
Gustav factory. This was
replaced soon afterwards by a
second version of the same
gun, which had a shorter
barrel, a very large trigger
guard, which could
accommodate gloved fingers in
winter, and a much straighter
stock than the original Finnish
gun; this gun was made by the
firm of Husqvarna. In the
course of World War II Sweden,
although neutral, increased her
army considerably to defend
herself if necessary and this led
to the realization that she had
no simple sub-machine gun for
mass-production. She set out
to rectify this but the result, the
Model 1945, was not in fact put
into production until after the
war. The Model 1945 was
made of stampings from heavy
gauge steel, riveted or welded
as necessary, and within the
limits imposed by these
methods was a sound and
reliable weapon.
Mechanically it bore a strong
resemblance to the British Sten
gun, but had a rectangular
stock of tubular metal which
could be folded forward on the
right of the gun without in any
way interfering with its working.
Although it was designed for
firing on automatic only, single
rounds could be fired by
anyone with a reasonably
sensitive trigger finger. It fired a
special high velocity cartridge,
and the original model used the
old Suomi fifty-round
magazine. Later versions fired
a new thirty-six round type but
as large stocks of the older

magazine, which was not
interchangeable, remained, the
new gun had an easily
detached magazine housing
which could be replaced by
one of the older type if
required. This was a temporary
provision only until adequate
supplies of the new magazine
became available, and the latest
models have riveted magazine
housings.

Above: *Swedish soldier with slung Carl Gustav Model 45 SMG; tubular stock folded forward.*

Left: *The 9mm Carl Gustav 45 is held in the firing position.*

Switzerland
REXIM-FAVOR

The history of this weapon is somewhat obscure. It was presented by the Turkish Army, attractively cased with a variety of accessories, to a senior British service officer attending an international rifle meeting in 1968. The Turks are not known to make sub-machine guns and there is no reason to suppose that it was locally made. The various inscriptions on the change lever and elsewhere are in the Turkish language but there is little doubt that it is one of the many varieties of the Swiss Rexim sub-machine gun which appeared from 1953 onwards, under the auspices of the Rexim Small Arms Company located in Geneva. It was at one time known as the Favor sub-machine gun, and is believed to have been made under contract by the Spanish Arsenal at Corunna. Extensive attempts were made in the mid-1950s to sell the Rexim in the Middle East, but there seems to be no record of any substantial deals being made, principally because the gun was considered to be too complicated, never a good recommendation for a sub-machine gun in which simplicity is almost the most important factor. The chief interest of the Rexim was that it fired from a closed bolt, that is, the round was fed into the chamber by the action of the cocking handle and remained there until pressure on the trigger allowed the firing pin to go forward. Motive power was provided by two coiled springs, one working inside the other with an intermediate hollow hammer, and looking exactly like an old-fashioned three-draw telescope. When the trigger was pressed the depression of the sear released the hammer which went forward under the force of the large outer spring, struck the firing pin, and fired the round. Normal blowback then followed and the cycle continued. The gun was well made, chiefly of pressings, but with a superior finish. It had a quick release barrel, in which the withdrawal of the small catch under the milled nut allowed the nut to be unscrewed and the barrel pulled out forward. In the model illustrated the butt had a separate pistol grip, presumably designed as a rear hand grip when using the short spring bayonet permanently attached to the muzzle. It took a magazine identical with that of the German MP40 gun. The gun illustrated is probably one of a small number purchased at some time by Turkey but never adopted for service.

United States of America
THOMPSON M1928A1

United States of America
THOMPSON M1A1

THOMPSON M1928A1

Length:	33.75" (857mm)
Weight:	10.75lb (4.88kg)
Barrel:	10.5" (267mm)
Calibre:	.45"
Rifling:	6 groove r/hand
Feed:	50 drum/20 box
C. Rate:	800 rpm
Muz Vel:	920 f/s (281 m/s)
Sights:	600 yds (549m)

THOMPSON M1A1

Length:	32.0" (813mm)
Weight:	10.45lb (4.74kg)
Barrel:	10.5" (267mm)
Calibre:	.45"
Rifling:	6 groove r/hand
Feed:	20/30-round box
C. Rate:	700 rpm
Muz Vel:	920 f/s (281 m/s)
Sights:	109 yds (100m)

Popularly associated with gangsters and terrorists, the Thompson served the Allies well in World War II. This 1928 model is shown with 20-round box magazine in place and 50-round drum at muzzle.

A World War II development of the famous "tommy gun" — a design almost a quarter of a century old by 1939-1945 — in which a straight forehand replaces the forward pistol grip.

United States of America
THOMPSON M1928A1

Some mention has already been made of the Thomspon sub-machine gun in the introduction to this section, since it was in many ways the most famous of all weapons of its type. It was developed in the course of World War I by Colonel (later Brigadier-General) J. T. Thompson but came too late to be used in action. Very few people wanted sub-machine guns after the war had ended so that the Auto-Ordnance Corporation which made them found it very difficult to keep going, particularly in the depression of the 1930s. Good advertising and publicity helped, however, and there was a small but steady sale to law enforcemnent agencies and also, regrettably but unavoidably, to criminals of various types. A surprising variety of models of the Thompson were made, almost all in .45″ calibre and one or two as automatic rifles rather than sub-machine guns. A few were even made in England by the Birmingham Small Arms Company. The weapon illustrated is the 1928, which with minor changes was the last peacetime version. The gun worked by the usual blowback system, but somewhat unusually in guns of this description it had a delay device to prevent the bolt from opening until the barrel pressure had dropped. Two squared grooves were cut into the sides of the bolt at an angle of 45°, the lower ends being nearer the face of the bolt, and an H-shaped bridge fitted into these. When the bolt was fully home the bottom ends of the H-piece engaged in recesses in the receiver. When the

Above: *A British soldier with a Thompson M1928A1 made by the Birmingham Small Arms Company.*

cartridge fired, the pressure was enough to cause it to rise, thus allowing the bolt to go back after a brief delay. This was hardly necessary in terms of safety but had the useful effect of slowing the cyclic rate which assisted accurate firing. The gun took either a fifty-round drum or a twenty-round box magazine, both of which are shown in the illustration.
A few of the guns may still be used by some US police forces.

United States of America
THOMPSON M1A1

The real breakthrough for the Thompson sub-machine gun came in 1938 when it was adopted by the United States Army. It was somewhat out of date and there were better weapons in existence but the Thompson was available and therefore accepted. Then the war came and the demand rose instantly. Apart from the domestic needs of the United States the main external purchaser was Great Britain who was glad enough to buy as many as she could be provided with in 1940. As with most

Above: *Hunting German stragglers at the war's end, the American nearest has an M1928 without forward grip.*

Left: *A policeman trains on the ranges in Honolulu, Hawaii, with his M1A1.*

other pre-war weapons the Thompson had been relatively luxuriously made and in view of the need to speed up production some simplification became essential. The first result was the M1 Type, the main mechanical difference being the abolition of the H-piece and the substitution of a heavier bolt to compensate for it. The main external differences were the absence of the compensator on the muzzle, the substitution of a straight forehand for the forward pistol grip (although this had been optional on the Model 28), the removal of the rather complex backsight, and its replacement by a simple flip. One main difference in functioning was that the new gun would not take the fifty-round drum, but as this had never been very reliable in dirty conditions it was no loss. A new thirty-round box magazine was introduced at the same time, and the earlier twenty-round magazine would also fit the new model. There was yet another simplification, the incorporation of a fixed firing pin on the face of the bolt; this resulted in the M1A1 which is the weapon illustrated. Although almost a quarter of a century old by then, the Thompson gave excellent service in 1939-45, for even if it was heavy to carry it was reliable and powerful.

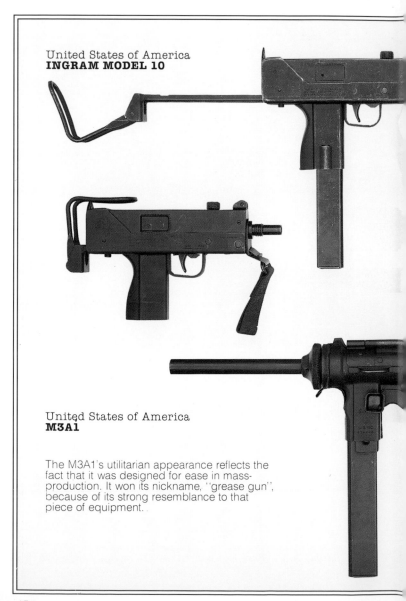

United States of America
INGRAM MODEL 10

United States of America
M3A1

The M3A1's utilitarian appearance reflects the fact that it was designed for ease in mass-production. It won its nickname, "grease gun", because of its strong resemblance to that piece of equipment.

M3A1

Length:	29.8'' (757mm)
Weight:	8.15lb (3.70kg)
Barrel:	8.0'' (203mm)
Calibre:	.45''
Rifling:	4 groove r/hand
Feed:	30-round box
C. Rate:	400 rpm
Muz Vel:	920 f/s (280 m/s)
Sights:	Fixed

INGRAM MODEL 10

Length:	10.5'' (267mm)
Weight:	7.63lb (3.46kg)
Barrel:	5.75'' (146mm)
Calibre:	.45'' or 9mm
Rifling:	6 groove r/hand
Feed:	30/32-round box
C. Rate:	1100 rpm
Muz Vel:	924 f/s (280 m/s)
Sights:	Fixed

The compact Ingram with its component parts of magazine and suppressor. Not very accurate it has nevertheless sold abroad to a number of countries.

United States of America
M3A1

In 1941 the Small Arms Development Branch of the United States Army Ordnance Corps set out to develop a sub-machine gun in accordance with certain guidelines proposed by the various combat arms. The intention was to produce a weapon which could be mass-produced by modern methods, and once the basic design had been established by George Hyde, a well-known expert in the field of sub-machine guns, the production side was put into the hands of Frederick Sampson, an expert of equal standing in his own field. A very detailed study of the methods used to manufacture the successful British Sten gun was also made, and the work went ahead so quickly that prototypes had been successfully tested well before the end of 1942, and the new weapon accepted as standard under the designation of M3. The new gun was a very utilitarian looking arm, made as far as possible from stampings and with practically no machining except for the barrel and bolt. It worked by blowback and had no provision for firing single rounds, but as its cyclic rate was low this was acceptable. Its stock was of retractable wire and the calibre was .45″ although conversion to 9mm was not difficult. It bore a strong resemblance to a grease gun, from which it derived its famous nickname. Large-scale use revealed some defects in the gun, and further successful attempts to simplify it were initiated; these resulted in the M3A1. Like its predecessor the new gun was made by modern

methods and was generally reliable. It worked, as before, by blowback but had no cocking handle, this process being achieved by the insertion of a finger into a slot cut in the receiver, by which the bolt could be withdrawn. The bolt, which had an integral firing pin, worked on guide rods which saved complicated finishing of the inside of the receiver and which gave smooth functioning with little interruption from dirt. An oil container was built into the pistol grip and a small bracket added to the rear of the retractable butt acted as a magazine filler. It used a box magazine which was not altogether reliable in dirty or dusty conditions until the addition of an easily removed plastic cover eliminated this defect. By the end of 1944 the new gun had been adopted and three months later it had officially replaced the Thompson as the standard sub-machine gun of the US Army.

Left: *A corporal from the United States Marine Corps carries his M3A1 slung under his equipment pack and ready for use against any enemy forces in the drop zone.*

United States of America
INGRAM MODEL 10

Named after its inventor, Gordon B. Ingram, this sub-machine gun evolved from a series of weapons designed after World War II. The Model 10 works on blowback but has wraparound bolts which make it possible to keep the weapon short and improve control at full automatic fire. The cocking handle on the top is equally convenient for right- or left-handed users. The magazine fits into the pistol-grip and the gun has a retractable butt. With the exception of the barrel it is made of stampings, with even the bolt made of sheet metal and filled with lead. The Model 10 is available in 9mm Parabellum or .45" Automatic Colt Pistol form. The smaller successor Model 11 variant differs mainly in the form of cartridge used, being the .38" ACP or 9mm Parabellum. Both are designed to be fitted with suppressors which can reduce sound considerably but are not conventional silencers because the bullet is allowed to reach its full velocity. It is a standard arm with a number of countries and was favoured by US special forces because of its handy size and high rate of fire; today, however, its inaccuracy is frowned upon and it is only produced in Model 11 form as the Cobray M11.

Left: *"Grease Gun" at the ready an American soldier in olive-green fatigues advances stealthily through wooded terrain anticipating a close-quarter encounter.*

Picture Credits

Unless otherwise credited, all pictures in this book were taken by Bruce Scott in the Weapons Museum, British School of Infantry, Warminister, Wiltshire.

The publisher wishes to thank the following organizations and individuals who have supplied photographs for this book. Photographs have been credited by page number; where more than one photograph appears on a page, references are made in the order of the columns across the page and then from top to bottom. The following abbreviations have been used: Bentham Literary Services (Colonel John Weeks): BLS; Imperial War Museum: IWM; Military Archive & Research Service, London: MARS. Additional research by Tony Moore.

6-7: Swiss Armeefotodienst; 8: National Army Museum/GKN Sankey; 10: ECPA; 11: US National Archives; 13: Bundesarchiv/US DoD; 14: US DoD; 15: Steyr Defence Products/Legion etrangere; 18-19: NATO; 22-23: ECPA; 23: Legion etrangere; 27: Terry Gander (2); 30-31: MARS; 34: IWM; 38: IWM; 42-43: IWM/Terry Gander/IWM; 44: UK Land Forces; 45: British Army Of the Rhine; 46-47: Accuracy International/Royal Ordnance; 48: Accuracy International; 49: UK Land Forces/British Aerospace; 54-55: Beretta/Israel Military Industries; 56: Stato Maggiore Dell'Esercito; 57: Israel Military Industries; 59: US Army; 64-65: US Army; 68: Salamander Books; 69: Finnish Embassy; 72-73: IWM; 76-77: MARS/Terry Gander (2); 78: IWM (2); 79: US Army; 82: IWM; 83: US DoD (2); 84-85: UK Land Forces; 86-87: IWM/Novosti Press Agency; 88: ECPA; 89: US Navy; 90: Heckler & Koch; 92: US Air Force; 93: US DoD; 97: Terry Gander; 100-101: MARS (2); 104: IWM; 105: Terry Gander; 107: Heckler & Koch; 108: IWM; 109: Salamander Books; 112-113: Terry Gander (2); 116: IWM; 117: Terry Gander; 120-121: Terry Gander (2); 124-125: BSA (2); 128: Central Office of Information, London; 129: Terry Gander; 133: Terry Gander; 136: Beretta; 144: Terry Gander; 145: IWM; 148: Terry Gander; 149: MARS; 152: IWM; 153: IWM/US Army; 156-157: US Marine Corps/US Army.

Bibliography

Weapons general		**Place and year of publication**	
Jane's Infantry Weapons	Weeks (Ed)	London	1979
Military Small Arms of the 20th Century	Hogg and Weeks	London	1977
Brasseys Infantry Weapons of the World	Owen (Ed)	London	1975
Small Arms of the World	Smith	London	1973
Illustrated Arsenal of the Third Reich	Normount	Wichenburg Arizona	1973
Arms and Armament	Ffoulkes	London	1945
The Soldier's Trade	Myatt	London	1974
British and American Infantry Weapons of World War II	Barker	London	1969
German Infantry Weapons of World War II	Barker	London	1969
Pistols, Rifles and Machine Guns	Allen	London	1953
Superiority of Fire	Pridham	London	1945
Small Arms Operation and Identification of Small Arms	Johnson (US Army Publication)	USA	1976
NATO Infantry and its Weapons	Owen (Ed)	London	1976
Warsaw Pact Infantry and its Weapons	Owen (Ed)	London	1976
Text-book for Small Arms	HMSO	London	1919
Text-book for Small Arms	HMSO	London	1929
Text-book of Ammunition	HMSO	London	1926

Note: Much use has been made of a variety of British and Foreign Military textbooks and pamphlets held in the Weapons Museum Reference Library, Warminster.

Sub-machine Guns			
The World's Sub-machine Guns	Nelson/Lockoven	London	1977
Pictorial History of the Sub-machine Gun	Hobart	London	1973

Rifles			
The Book of the Rifle	Fremantle	London	1901
The Englishman and the Rifle	Cottesloe	London	1945
The Book of Rifles	Smith	Harrisburgh Pa	1965
The Lee-Enfield Rifle	Reynolds	London	1960
Remarks on the Rifle (11th Ed)	Baker	London	1935
English Guns and Rifles	George	London	1947

OTHER SUPER-VALUE MILITARY GUIDES IN THIS SERIES

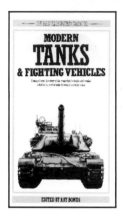

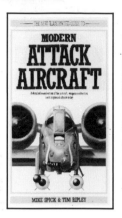

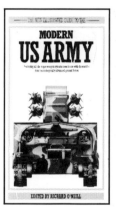

OTHER ILLUSTRATED MILITARY GUIDES AVAILABLE

Modern US Fighters and Attack Aircraft
Modern US Navy
Modern Warships
Aircraft Markings
Allied Fighters of World War II

★ Each title has 160 fact-filled pages
★ Each is colorfully illustrated with hundreds of action photographs and technical drawings
★ Each contains concisely presented data and accurate descriptions of major international weapons systems
★ Each title represents tremendous value for money

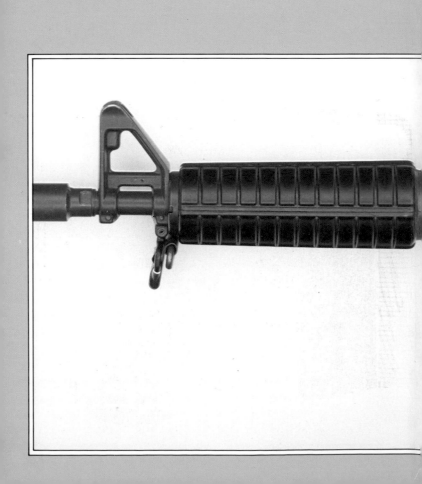